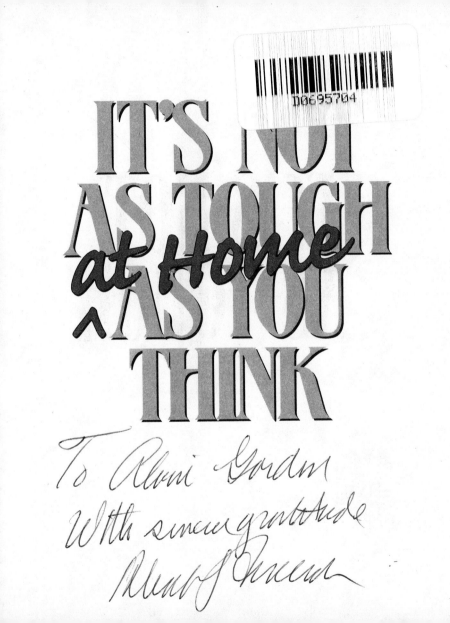

IT'S NOT AS TOUGH *at Home* ^AS YOU THINK

To Alvin Gordon
With sincere gratitude

[signature]

IT'S NOT
AS TOUGH

A
SHAAR
PRESS
PUBLICATION

at Home
^AS YOU THINK

Making Family Life Smoother and Better

RABBI ABRAHAM J. TWERSKI, M.D.

TABLE OF CONTENTS

1.

DOES EVERYONE HAVE PROBLEMS?

It is easy for me to assume that problems are universal. As a psychiatrist, people do not consult me to tell me how happy they are. Day in, day out I am presented with a variety of emotional and psychological problems. It is easy to conclude that the whole world is one great big problem.

O.K. Not everyone has problems. Yet, we cannot escape the impression that there are many more problems today than in the past. There may be a valid reason for this. Problems occur against a background. If you develop a nagging headache or cough at home or at work, you are aware of the discomfort and you have a problem. If your house is on fire and you are trying to save yourself and rescue everyone in the house, you are totally unaware that your head hurts or that you are coughing. A certain level of comfort must exist in order to be able to identify *dis*comfort.

I don't think mankind has ever before experienced as radical a change in lifestyle in so short a period of time as we have.

1

Earlier this century, the average life span was *under forty*. Today it is twice that and increasing. In 1917 the flu epidemic killed hundreds of thousands of people. Today, with antibiotics and vaccines, major epidemics are rare. Just several decades ago, work often entailed physical exhaustion. Today most work is done by machines and by computers. In the past there was no escape from sweltering heat. Today we can be comfortable indoors in the most intense heat wave. The miraculous progress of medical science and technology has revolutionized our lives. We can now be much more comfortable than in the past. Against a background of comfort, discomfort is more likely to be felt.

I can testify that in the 1940s parents and children did not have the luxury of worrying about some behavior problems. They were preoccupied by the fear of polio. Every muscle ache triggered anxiety that the child might have this crippling disease.

The marvels of scientific progress have resulted in our feeling that life should be comfortable. We are less prepared to deal with discomfort. Young people share in this attitude. When they encounter discomfort, there is the risk that they will resort to chemicals that promise to make them feel better. After all, when grownups don't feel as relaxed as they would like to, they take tranquilizers. Kids may go for other tranquilizers, like alcohol or drugs.

We need to establish an attitude in the home that, all the marvels of science notwithstanding, the goal of life is *not* the achievement of maximum comfort. The goal of life is to achieve *something*, hopefully spirituality and character development. It would certainly help if parents would not resort to alcohol or tranquilizers when dealing with normal stresses.

Parents should establish a value system in the home. The children should feel that each individual and the family as a whole has a mission. It is much easier to tolerate some discomfort if you are heading toward a goal. If the purpose of life is to achieve maximum comfort, every little discomfort can become a major problem.

We are the beneficiaries of unprecedented conveniences in living. These are indeed wonderful. This may lead to an attitude that no one should have to tolerate any inconvenience at all. We should avail ourselves of spiritual teachings that can help us understand why we must sometimes bear inconveniences. If we are really convinced of this, we are more likely to convey it to our children.

Please notice that the title of this book is not "Life Is Not Tough." Rather it is "It's Not As Tough As You Think." In other words, life does not have to be paralyzingly tough. We can smooth out some of the bumps in life. But it is unrealistic to think that all rough spots can be eradicated. We must still do much coping. Our intent is to encourage you to cope. If a situation appears to be overwhelmingly tough, don't just give up. If it can be broken down to bite size, it can be dealt with successfully.

2.

CHANGE REQUIRES CHANGE

Human beings are creatures of habit. We do things a certain way for a long period of time and then if we must change our pattern, considerable effort and attention are required. This is true even if the change is for the better. Suppose you have been driving a car that has the gear-shift lever on the steering wheel shaft and then you upgrade to a luxury sports car that has the gear-shift lever between the seats. You are driving a much better car, but chances are that at the beginning you will be turning on the windshield wipers each time you try to shift gears. You will have to concentrate on shifting rather than doing it automatically. This is true of all changes.

Think of the family as a system. The system is very much like a mobile — you know, the toy that hangs over the baby's crib, with little figurines suspended from a central pole. When it is not in motion, all the pieces rest in one position at an equilibrium. If you move any one figurine ever so slightly, the equilibrium has been upset and all the others must now shift to a new position to establish a new equilibrium.

Much the same is true of a family or any group system. All the members of a group have been functioning in a way that maintained the equilibrium. If any one member changes in any way, every other member must accommodate to establish a new equilibrium. As we noted, change requires concentration and effort. Sometimes the change may require so much energy output that the group may try to reestablish the old equilibrium, even if it were less desirable.

Change can be of any kind. A child may go off to school in another city. A child may marry and leave home, or bring his spouse home. There may be a new baby in the family. All these may be very desirable, but they require accommodation by everyone else. If any member of the family is going to try to live exactly as he did before, there is likely to be some turbulence.

I have seen cases where a wife complained bitterly about her alcoholic husband. However, if the husband recovers, it is not unusual to find that the joy over his recovery is marred by some dissatisfaction. Everyone had been accustomed to behaving with an active alcoholic in the family. The sober person has created a change, and the natural resistance to change may result in the unwitting undermining of his recovery.

Whether the change is for the better or not, a family should realize that when there is a change, it is not going to be business as usual. The transition to a new equilibrium can be smooth if it is anticipated. If any difficulty arises, the family members can discuss it among themselves and work out the new accommodation. Sometimes there may be a need for counseling to assist in the readjustment.

Readjustments may be tough on some members of the family. With preparation and a bit of help, it does not have to be as tough as you think.

3.

MORE GIVE THAN TAKE

The ideal relationship is where each partner wants to give more to the union than he/she wants to take from it. When the reverse is true, frustrations at not having one's desires satisfied are likely to occur. This is rare when there is more giving than taking. This attitude between parents makes a profound impression upon the children. The reduction in sibling rivalry can be a palpable blessing.

There are many relationships where this is indeed the case. These are indeed happy relationships. Both partners are supportive of each other. Both are able to withstand stress much better. Abuse is virtually impossible when the other partner's happiness is the foremost consideration.

That is the kind of marriage I witnessed at home. I will cite just one incident that sheds light on the nature of the relationship.

My father was diagnosed with cancer of the pancreas that had spread to the liver. From his many years of visiting the sick and discussing their cases with their doctors, he had a better than average knowledge of medicine.

"You know that cancer of the pancreas that has affected the liver does not respond to chemotherapy. Right?" he said. I agreed.

"Then there is no point in undergoing a treatment which can have very unpleasant side effects if there is nothing to be gained from it. Right?" Again I agreed.

"Then we both understand that there will be no chemotherapy," he said. "O.K.," I responded.

However, the doctor had told my mother that there was very little to expect from chemotherapy. At the very best, he said, it could extend my father's life three months.

"Three months!" my mother exclaimed. "Why, even three days is precious. Every additional day of life must be preserved." She then told my father that he must undergo chemotherapy.

"I'm sorry the doctor said what he did," my father said to me. "I know that chemotherapy will do nothing except make me miserable.

"But," my father went on, "if I refuse chemotherapy, then when I die, mother may feel guilty. She may say, 'If only I had insisted on chemotherapy, he might still have lived.' I don't want mother to feel guilty. I'll take the therapy. I've done many things for mother during our 52 years together. This gives me the chance to do one last thing."

This was the nature of their marriage. This is the kind of stuff that good relationships are made of.

4.

HUGGING IS NUTRITIOUS

When I saw a bumper sticker saying "Have you hugged your kids today?" my initial reaction was, "What kind of foolish question is that?" That's like saying, "Have you breathed today?" Then I realized that it is not at all foolish. There are children who do not get enough hugs.

Children need hugging. Extensive research has shown that infants who do not get enough human touching and caressing may become chronically depressed.

When my children were little, my parents visited. My father got down on the floor to play with his grandchildren. My mother's eyes welled up with tears. "I never had that," she said. "We stood in awe of our father. It would have been sacrilege to hug and kiss him. We only kissed the back of his hand, as with giving obeisance."

My father lived near his grandfather. Virtually every night, his grandfather would visit before the children went to sleep. He would play with them a moment, tickle them under the arm, kiss them gently and send them to bed. That is probably why my father could get down on the floor with my children.

This behavior may be transmitted generationally. If you hug your kids, they will hug theirs. Everybody will be healthier.

Make it a practice to hug your children the moment you come home from work. If you delay, your wife may tell you how the child misbehaved. At that point a hug might be interpreted as sanctioning bad behavior. So hug them before you might have to discipline them.

Let the children know you love them. If disciplining should be necessary, it will be more effective.

5.

POTHOLE ALERT

You know what it's like when spring comes. You feel like you need a Sherman tank to make it across town. The repeated freezing and thawing has resulted in the roads being pock-marked with potholes. Some seem to rival the Grand Canyon in depth. Countless hubcaps have been lost and wheels thrown out of alignment. Why don't they fix these things?

Well, as soon as they start fixing them, other problems arise. Now you have lanes closed by the construction crews, and you seem to be eternally delayed by the flagmen. If they must resurface the entire road, you have to take complicated detours. If the detour signs are not posted properly, you may end up miles from your destination.

If they can send people to the moon, can't they develop a concrete that won't form potholes?

The road through family living may also be marred by potholes. There may be arguments and "freezes." Although the freezes thaw out and everyone seems to be on good terms, emotional "potholes" may remain. Yes, these potholes can be fixed, and the whole relationship may even be resurfaced. As with traffic, these may come at a considerable cost.

We cannot control the external weather, but there is much that we can do about the internal weather. We can prevent "freezes." If we feel we must criticize, we should do so gently and in the same manner we would wish to be corrected. If we are the recipients of criticism, we should listen patiently and give some thought to what the other person says. We should then be able to respond in a rational manner. If we become defensive we may lash out in retaliation. Perhaps we may elect not to respond at all, giving the other person the "silent treatment." This may constitute a freeze. After several days, the relationship may warm up, and we may think that all has been forgotten and forgiven. Not necessarily so. The thaw may result in a "pothole."

Empathy, consideration, and giving the other person the benefit of the doubt may help avoid potholes. Open communication, with respect for the other person even when disagreeing, can prevent the freeze. If there is no freezing, it is unlikely that there will be potholes. One can then navigate the road through life relatively smoothly, without being thrown out of alignment.

6.

IT'S THE LAW

We know we cannot defy the law of gravity. Whatever goes up must come down whether you like it or not.

There are some laws which are not really physical laws of nature, but for all intents and purposes, they might as well be. They appear as immutable as the physical ones.

For example, there is a physical law of nature that a gas will expand to fill the size of the container. In a little container, the gas will be compressed. In a large container it will spread out to fill the container. The analogy is that stuff will accumulate to fill the drawers you have. If you add a chest of drawers, it too will soon be filled with stuff. Where was this stuff stored before you acquired the new chest? That remains an unsolved mystery.

Similarly, if you add a piece of furniture to the room, it will become a resting place for hats, books, briefcases, and what not. Where did these land before the new piece was added? Again, a mystery.

The point of this is that you should not have the expectation that once you add a chest of drawers or an end table, there will now be less cluttering and more room in other drawers. This does not happen, and if you expect it to, you will be disappointed.

What about timesaving devices? Will you have more spare time now that you have a microwave oven and a dishwasher? Forget it. Much like gas that expands to fill the container, the things you have to do will expand to fill whatever time is available.

Just accept these ancillary "laws of nature." You will be spared considerable frustration and disappointment.

7.

LET THE BEES BE

You might think of the perfect family as one in which the children do no wrong. They always listen to the parents. Siblings never fight. Husband and wife never quarrel. Peace and tranquility reign. The ideal family, right?

Wrong! The family is the place where children should be prepared for the world of reality. The world is hardly one of peace and tranquility. Children growing up in an "ideal" family would be totally unprepared for real life, just as a child raised in a sterile "bubble" would not develop any immunity and would succumb to the first contact with germs. The many challenges in the normal family may be unpleasant, but this is where children train for life in the real world.

A friend of mine had a farm with many fruit trees. As a result he had no peace from the bees. His wife complained that she panics when sunbathing. So he decided to get rid of the pesky bees.

The following spring the trees were covered with beautiful blossoms, but produced no fruit. Blossoms develop into fruit only if there are bees that carry the pollen from one blossom to another. No bees, no fruit.

We should realize that some annoyances might actually be productive learning experiences for family members. Siblings fight, then make up. Children disobey and are disciplined. Husband and wife disagree, then come to an acceptable compromise. These may be unpleasant, but so are bees. Unpleasant, but essential. This should make some of the altercations in the family a bit easier to tolerate.

8.

MEMORIES NEVER SPOIL

In *Generation to Generation* I pointed out that the statement "diamonds are forever" is not quite true. They are indeed long lasting, but they can be lost. Memories cannot be lost. Memories are really forever. If you wish to give someone a precious gift, give memories.

The family is the place where memories can abound. Every enjoyable experience shared with family members can be retained forever. You can show your great-grandchildren pictures that were taken on vacation when their grandparents were tots. You can relive the vacation, and perhaps remind your children (their grandparents) how you nearly went out of your mind when they wandered off at age 5 and got lost in the forest. Now you can laugh at what was once the most terrifying experience in your life.

There are memories of holidays celebrated together and of joyous family affairs. You may be surprised that your children may come up with vivid recollections of things that occurred when they were 3!

The comic-strip character "Ziggy" is a person who rarely has anything good happen to him. But look here! Ziggy is smiling. Perhaps his present circumstances are not that great, but no one can deprive him of the memories of the good things that did occur.

There is something else about memories. They are the bonds that tie the generations together. In this fragmented world where virtually everything becomes obsolete within a brief period of time (including a $45,000 luxury automobile), family memories are one of the few things that can have durability. This can provide a feeling of security unachievable by any other means.

When family members get together, photo albums come out. You probably have some pictures of people you don't recognize. Then someone will say, "Oh, that's Aunt Bella or cousin Bennie!" You write the name on the back of the photo. The identification might be followed by some information about these relatives. You will learn more about the family. Everyone present is interested, to one degree or another, in the pictures. Of course, if it's your or your children's wedding album, going over the pictures has special significance.

I'm sure you have some very fine friends. But just how interested do you think they will be in your family pictures? There is no substitute for family members, even distant ones, to share cherished memories.

If you are able to, you will set aside some money for your children's education. That is indeed important. One day that money will have been used up. The experiences you give them that will generate pleasant memories will provide them with a gift from which they can benefit all their lives.

Ziggy is right. Memories never spoil, and they are never used up.

9.

GRATITUDE CAN MITIGATE SADNESS

We were sitting at a wedding banquet when cousin Evie's eyes welled up with tears. She rose and left the table. We all knew why. This was the first wedding she was attending unaccompanied by Martin. He died six months earlier, just one week short of their 55th wedding anniversary, which was to have been a gala affair.

When Evie returned I said to her, "Evie, go over to the bride and tell her you can promise her 55 years of happiness if she will sign on the dotted line. What do you think she'll do?"

"Of course she'll sign," Evie said. "I would have, too."

"Then you had what many people could only wish for. Of course it would have been better if you had had Martin for 60 years. But be reasonable," I said. "Be thankful for those many years."

That broke the ice. Evie smiled and began recalling some pleasant memories. We chimed in, and soon we were all laughing. Evie even became relaxed enough to mention a few of Martin's habits at which she had been peeved.

Losing a spouse is a huge, huge bump. We could not relieve Evie's loneliness. But as she became aware of her gratitude for having 55 years with her husband, the pain over his loss was assuaged a bit.

Gratitude is a positive feeling. Sadness is a negative feeling. The two cannot coexist any more than can light and darkness.

When someone suffers a loss, family members may be in a position to bring some comfort. Gratitude for having had a loving relationship cannot compensate for the loss, but it *can* mitigate the sadness and the pain.

10.

GOOD NEIGHBOR, GOOD FRIEND

When I was an intern, I shared a room in the hospital quarters with another intern. Some nights I worked all night and dropped off to sleep at dawn. A few hours later my roommate would come in and turn on the radio. "Bert," I said, "please don't turn on the radio when you see I'm asleep." It did not help. He no sooner entered the room than he turned on the radio full blast.

I had no other choice. I removed a tube from the radio. (Those were the days when you took a broken radio to be repaired.) "I will have to take it down to the repair shop," Bert said. After he left the room, I put the tube back. "I can't understand it," Bert said. "It played perfectly good at the repair shop." The next time he woke me with the radio, I did it again. "Something's weird with this radio," Bert said.

I had to confess. "There's nothing weird with the radio," I said. "There's something weird about a guy who is inconsiderate and turns the radio on loud when someone in the room is sleeping." Bert finally got the message.

Family members are not the only ones who should be thoughtful of one another. Sharing a room, an apartment, or a house demands consideration.

When Rabbi Shlomo Zalman Auerbach was old and weak, he emerged from the synagogue in Jerusalem and was approached by a man who said he had a serious problem. The rabbi's aide tried to shoo the man away, since the rabbi was not feeling well. "No, no," Rabbi Auerbach said. "When someone has a problem, you must listen."

The man said, "I live in an upper flat. My carpet is dirty, so I rolled it up. I can't afford to get it cleaned. My downstairs neighbor says he can hear my footsteps and it bothers him. Am I obligated to keep the carpet on the floor?"

"Of course," the rabbi said. "You must be considerate of your neighbor. Cleaning your carpet need not be costly. You can get some carpet-cleaning solution at the hardware store and clean it yourself. But you may not cause your neighbor any discomfort."

The fact is that I am more impressed by the rabbi's insistence on hearing the problem in his weakened state than by the actual answer. But the latter is indeed important. Even if you are not related, you must be considerate of anyone with whom you share a dwelling.

The Talmud states that a person must be a good friend and a good neighbor (*Ethics of the Fathers* 2:13). You cannot be a good friend if you are not a good neighbor.

11.

WALKING A TIGHTROPE

It's like walking a tightrope. You must keep a delicate balance. There is not too much room to err on either side.

If we don't expect much of others, they may not be stimulated adequately to perform optimally. If we expect too much from them, they may not perform at all. "What's the use? I cannot satisfy them anyway."

This is especially true with children. It's not unheard of for a child to bring home a test paper with a grade of 96. A parent may say, "Why didn't you get 100?" Parents may actually be a bit peeved if a friend's child was valedictorian while their child came in second as salutatorian. Reasonable expectations can be stimulating. Excessive demands may stifle performance.

Some students suffer from exam anxiety. Although they know the material well, their mind goes blank when they take the exam. This is because they invest the exam with inordinate importance. A poor grade would not be just a setback. It would be total devastation. If there is too much riding on what you are trying to do, the anxiety and fear of failure may so paralyze you that you are bound to fail. I call this the "William Tell Syndrome."

There is a story about a famous archer, William Tell, who offended the king by refusing to lift his hat when the king passed by. As a punishment, the king ordered William Tell to shoot an arrow at an apple perched on his son's head. (The story ends with William Tell successfully hitting the apple. He then says to the king, "If I had harmed my son, the next arrow would have been for you.")

I am a very poor archer. If I were told to try and hit the bull's-eye, I might, with some luck, get close to it. My hand would be steady, because if I missed the target it would not be any big deal. But if I were told to aim at an apple perched on my child's head, I would be doomed to fail. Why? Because the dread consequences of not hitting the apple would cause me such great anxiety that my hands would tremble. No way could I aim properly.

If children are made to feel that their worth depends on excelling in performance, the pressure to succeed may be so great that it renders them incapable of using their skills. They may be fully capable of doing whatever the task is. However, the dread of failure may paralyze them.

Parental love should be unconditional. In *Generation to Generation* I cited the custom in some families that with the birth of each additional child, the mother adds a candle to the kindling of the Sabbath eve lights. When I found out that my mother had added a candle when I was born, I was thrilled. It meant that my existence had made our house a bit brighter. The increased brightness did not depend on my grades. The house was just as bright when I scored 70 as it was when I scored 100.

If parents do not expect good performance from a child, he may conclude that they consider him inept. If he knows that they do expect him to do well, but that they will love him just as much if he does not excel, he will not be threatened by the possibility of failure.

As much as we wish to reassure our children that we love them even if their performance is not up to par, we must be careful not to reward failure.

PEANUTS reprinted by permission of United Feature Syndicate, Inc.

Marcie is right. Peppermint Patty's father should have told her that he loves her even though she made poor grades. Rewarding her for this may encourage her to fail again.

Our love for our children should not require any intellectual calculation. But we should give some thought as to how we react to their performance.

12.

AWAY FROM HOME AT HOME

Amother complained to a psychologist about her son's behavior. "Why does he behave better when he is in someone else's home?" The psychologist responded, "Madam, don't you?"

Of course we act differently at home. We may dress casually, and we can speak in a more relaxed manner. After all, home is the place where one should feel at ease.

One can feel at ease and relaxed while maintaining an attitude of propriety and respect. Especially today, when society has done away with so many inhibitions, acting with reverence in the home is especially important.

It is perfectly O.K. to be more casual at home. However, respect and consideration should not fall by the wayside because of familiarity. Self-control and courtesy are at least as important at home as elsewhere. Yelling is as out of place at home as when you are someone's guest.

You probably say "thank you" to the waiter, even though you pay for the food and leave a tip. You don't pay for the food at home nor do you tip your mother. Doesn't she deserve a "thank you" when she serves your food? By the same token, parents should thank children for things they do.

An excellent guide to proper action at home is the awareness that one is always in the presence of G-d. If one would act with reverence in the presence of an important personage, how much more so in the presence of G-d.

A sage was riding in a horse-drawn coach which passed a field with bales of hay. The driver alighted and said to his passenger, "I'm going to help myself to a few bales of hay. Keep an eye out, and if you see someone watching, tell me quickly."

Just as the driver was about to take the first bale, the sage said, "Someone's watching!" The driver quickly jumped onto the coach and sped away. "Thank you for warning me," he said, "but I didn't see anyone." "You couldn't have seen Him," the sage said. "You told me to tell you if someone was watching, and indeed, G-d is watching."

Our dress, our speech, and all our behavior within the four walls of our home should be such that we would feel good if someone were watching.

Some people think that maintaining proper decorum at home is tough. It's not as tough as you think. Either make believe you're at someone else's home, or at the very least behave in a way that would make you feel good if someone were watching.

PROTECTIVE WALLS CAN BE A PRISON

hilip and Doris consulted me because they felt that their marriage of six months was beginning to deteriorate. They could not understand why this was happening. They had a wonderful courtship and anticipated a blissful marriage. But Philip was becoming distant and seclusive. He began coming home late from work, and his attitude toward Doris was cool. This was so different from what they had expected. Something was wrong, but they did not know what.

It turned out that Philip had what I refer to as a "compartmentalized" negative self-concept. Some people have unwarranted global feelings of inferiority. I.e., they have a distorted self-image as a result of which they think of themselves as unlikable and inadequate in every way. Some people have a partial self-image distortion. I.e., they know that they are adequate and competent in some ways, but they think of themselves as inferior in other ways.

Philip was a brilliant physicist and was generally well-read. He knew he was bright, and was able to bedazzle people with his intelligence. However, except for this quality, he thought of himself as having nothing to offer. He felt that as a person there was nothing about him to like.

During their courtship, Philip could impress Doris with his brilliance. In the rather brief encounters of dating, he did not feel uncomfortable because there was little chance that Doris would see through the superficial veneer of his intellectuality. His display of cleverness was an act to cover up what he felt was his real self, an emotionally dull and insipid person.

Once they were married, Philip began to feel uneasy. This was no longer a relationship of a few hours several times a week. This was going to be constant contact, seven days a week. There was no way he could keep up a facade indefinitely. Sooner or later Doris would get a sense of what he felt was his "real" self, and she would certainly not be pleased with that. Why, she might even want out of the marriage! The only way he could preserve the marriage was to prevent Doris from really getting to know him. He therefore began building a protective wall around himself. This is why he distanced himself from her. He stayed away from home a good deal, and when he was home he was aloof. Philip felt threatened by the very intimacy he desired.

Fortunately, Philip was able to accept this interpretation, and after some individual and group therapy geared toward enhancing self-esteem, he became much less defensive. Their marriage then blossomed.

People who have unwarranted feelings of inferiority may build walls around themselves to defend their fragile egos. Alas! These walls are both a barrier and a prison.

People who feel uncomfortable in an intimate relationship should seek counseling. They are very likely suffering unnecessarily because of a distorted self-concept. A true self-awareness will reward them with happiness.

14.

NO ONE IS PERFECT

One of the most severe "bumps" in life is when parents have a child who has limitations. Sometimes these are of the kind that will never allow the child to find his place in a culture that measures a person's value by his productivity.

It would be ideal if we could separate economic and industrial values from personal values. Our society is so preoccupied with the criteria of success in business that we tend to measure human value by how much a person can achieve or produce. People who are unable to meet these criteria may not be highly valued.

Let us think the way one mother did. She had a child who was born with several defects. She said, "When I sit in the rocking chair cradling my baby in my arms, I see how he is different. I know how much I love this child with all his shortcomings. That is when I can understand how much G-d can love me with all my shortcomings."

None of us is perfect. Granted, there are levels of imperfection. This mother's wise words apply not only to G-d, but to other people as well. We are often judged by the way we judge. If we value others in spite of their imperfections, we are likely to be judged similarly by others.

15.

BE A PARENT, NOT A PAL

"**B**e a pal to your child." This may be good advice up to a point. Children should always feel that their parents are friends. But let's remember. There are millions of people from whom children can choose friends. There are only two people in the entire world who can be their parents. Becoming a "pal" to your children at the cost of compromising your role as a parent can deprive them of a vital and irreplaceable resource.

There are some parents who feel that getting down to their children's level at any time would undermine their position of authority. They point out that a king does not play tennis with his subjects. I don't believe that this is valid. Parents can hike with their children and play ball or other games with them. However, they should remember that they are parents, not peers.

When kids play baseball and one player drops the ball or strikes out with the bases loaded, other kids may vent their anger on him. It probably would be better if they would handle the situation more gingerly. However, no great harm is done if they use some choice words to express their disappointment at losing the game. If dad happens to be the player whose error resulted in the game being lost, children must remember that they must retain their respect for father. "That's the last time you're going to be on *our* team, Dad," is acceptable. "Dad, you stink!" is not acceptable.

Democracy is probably the best system of government available, but the family is not a democratic system. For that matter, neither is a football team. The quarterback calls the plays. There are systems where there must be an authority. Parents should not be despots who stifle any expression of opinion that may disagree with theirs. They should welcome their children's input, but they must retain the authority.

Yes, there are ways in which you can be a "pal" to your child, but never relinquish your role as parent.

16.

BUT WHERE DO I ATTACH THE HORSES?

We've heard it a number of times. A person essentially says. "Don't bother me with logic. My mind is made up."

Many difficulties result when a person does not want to listen to reason. That's the way we are when our minds are made up. In the interest of harmony within the home, I appeal to you to keep an open mind. If you are really right, you can conclude that after considering all the pros and cons. If you are not right, why should you want to maintain a wrong position?

My father told a story of the villagers who were told about a locomotive that pulls wagons without horses. They were in disbelief. Wagons cannot move unless they are pulled by horses! Everyone knows that. However, upon hearing repeated reports of this phenomenon, they sent a representative to the big city to see for himself and bring back a report.

The representative returned with a confirmation of the rumor. It was really true! Wagons moved without horses! He then explained at great length how a locomotive works. He drew diagrams of the steam container, and showed how the steam pressure pushes against a piston that causes the wheels to turn. One by one the villagers grasped the principle of this marvelous phenomenon.

All except one. One villager arose and protested. "Have you all gone insane?" he asked. "For thousands of years wagons have been pulled by horses, and now things have suddenly changed? This representative must have been hypnotized to think he saw wagons moving on their own, and you are foolish enough to believe something so absurd!"

By this time the other villagers had grasped the principle of the steam engine. They all descended on this non-believer, and laboriously explained how the steam engine could make the wheels turn. He ultimately conceded.

Just before the meeting was to dissolve, the skeptic raised his hand. "I understand everything perfectly. The steam, the pressure, the piston, everything. I have only one question. On that diagram of the locomotive, I don't see where you attach the horses!"

That's the way it sometimes is. We listen, nod approval, and may agree with others. But after all is said and done, we stand obstinately by our previous opinion.

As human beings, we pride ourselves on our intelligence. Obstinacy does not require intelligence. Let's keep an open mind and give logic a try.

17.

ACT ANGRY BUT DON'T BE ANGRY

nger is destructive. It's bad for high blood-pressure and migraine headaches. There are books and audio-tapes on managing anger. It's no small trick to condition yourself so that the blood does not rush to your head when provoked. But it's all in your favor if you can do this.

Children often do things that can enrage you. They must be taught not to repeat these actions. It is a mistake to be overly tolerant. They must be prepared for living in society, and society is not going to be as tolerant of their misbehavior as you may be.

Some books on parenting say, "Don't shout at your children when you are angry," to which Erma Bombeck responded, "When am I supposed to shout at them? When they kiss me on Mother's Day?"

If discipline requires shouting at them to get the point across (it's not always necessary), then you should shout, *but not while you are angry*. Leave the room for a few moments, walk around the house, or take a mouthful of water and see how long you can hold it. Wait until your initial rage reaction subsides. Then, if you must shout, go ahead. Even then, try to lower the decibels.

Why? Because if you shout at the height of your anger you may say unwise things. You may call the child "stupid" or some other derogatory term. You might lose control and hit him. Remember, condemn the *behavior*, not the *child*.

If you wait until your anger has subsided, you will have much better control, and your reaction can be constructive.

What should you do if you did lose your cool and say things you wish you had not said? Apologize, of course. You may say, "Son, what you did was wrong and I don't want you to ever do that again. I'm sorry I lost my cool. I love you and I just don't want you to do things that are harmful to yourself or others."

Apologizing is a very good way to teach a child that losing one's cool is wrong.

18.

THE PITFALLS OF PRAISE

hildren need positive strokes. In *It's Not As Tough As You Think* I pointed out that flattery is not a positive stroke. Praise elevates a child's self-esteem only when it is true.

My 7-year-old grandson came to me with his violin, on which he had taken four lessons. "*Zeide* (grandfather), do you want to hear me play?" "Of course," I said.

He proudly took the fiddle out of its case, put some resin on the bow, and began playing "Twinkle, twinkle, little star." If you have ever heard a 7-year-old play the violin after just several lessons, you know what it sounded like. He was proud of his achievement, and I was about to say, "Wow, that's beautiful," when I caught myself. That was not true. It was not beautiful.

I'm convinced that we really cannot lie successfully. At least I can't. We have body language and non-verbal communication over which we have no control. When we lie, we send a conflicting and garbled message. We say one thing, our bodies say another. The recipient gets both of the messages. False compliments are recognized, at some level of perception, as being false.

I said to my grandson, "I recognize that tune" (which was true). "Play it again and I'll sing it along with you." He did, and I did, and he was beaming. I had acknowledged his playing and did not lie.

Similarly, when a child does something which deserves praise, we should comment on the act. "It was very thoughtful of you to let Jerry ride your bike." The statement, "You are really a wonderful boy for letting Jerry ride your bike," is not wise. He may have grudgingly let Jerry ride the bike, and at this moment he may hate Jerry. He does not think of himself as being wonderful. He may be thinking, "If they only knew that I hope Jerry falls off the bike and breaks his leg, they wouldn't think I am so wonderful." Praising the act instead of the person eliminates this pitfall.

Praising children is important. We just need to be a bit cautious how we do it.

19.

EACH DAY IS A NEW DAY

There is probably nothing as destructive to a marriage, or for that matter, to all family relationships, as allowing oneself to become bored with other family members. People who are thrill-seekers and who find their relationship to have become routine may think that another relationship will provide the excitement they seek.

I don't like to inject a note of sadness, but sometimes we do not value something unless we realize we may lose it. Each day we have our parents, spouse, siblings, and children should be a new day. They are a gift to us today.

I had a wonderful relationship with my older brother, but we lived miles apart and would meet only at family gatherings. We would then go over old times and laugh together about things that happened years ago. We would remind each other about the people we knew in our childhood. It was great fun.

I no longer have my older brother. I can remember the events and the people, but the fun is gone. There is no one with whom

I can share these memories. In a world with several billion people, there is not a single human being who can remember the things my brother and I were able to share. I regret that we only met two or three times a year. One aspect of my life has become lonely. This particular loneliness can never be remedied.

Everyone in the family is one of a kind. No one is replaceable.

On many of the packaged foods we buy, the ingredients may include, "xxx added to maintain freshness." We should add such "chemicals" to our relationships.

People may become bored with me only if I am the same person today that I was yesterday. If there is something new about me, I will be "fresh" to them. If we make it our business to grow in some way each day, we are likely to maintain our freshness. In *Growing Each Day* I suggested ways in which we can enhance our spirituality each day.

We may become more interesting not only to others, but to ourselves as well.

20

CLEAR THE CLUTTER

Psychologists have not yet figured out why some people collect certain things. I don't mean like stamps and coins. Those are excellent hobbies. I mean like absolutely worthless blown-out fuses that can be found atop fuse boxes, little jars that have been sitting in the cupboard for seven years awaiting some use, or useless parts of games or toys that have long since been discarded. Men, women, and children all save useless stuff.

Other than taking up some room, these collectibles are rather innocent. I mean, what would you use the space atop the fuse box for if the blown-out fuses were not there? Whereas accumulating useless stuff is rather harmless, there is one place where cluttering is definitely harmful: the brain.

We marvel at the acuteness of memory of youngsters. As we grow older, we may not be able to remember the name of the person who has lived next door to us for the past 14 years. Why is that?

I think that this phenomenon was best explained by Sherlock Holmes. Dr. Watson was astonished to discover that Holmes was ignorant of the Copernican theory that the earth revolves around the sun rather than the reverse. He was even more flabbergasted when Holmes said that now that he knew it, he would do his best to forget it.

Holmes explained that his concept of the human mind was that it was like a chest with many compartments for storage. Some minds may have more compartments, others less. However, all minds have a finite number of empty spaces into which one may place data. When all the spaces have been filled, you cannot put anything more in unless you make room for it by emptying a compartment.

It is therefore important, Holmes said, to avoid storing data for which one has no use. Such data will preclude having space for storing useful data. Inasmuch as how the sun and planets move is irrelevant to his function, there was no point in his keeping that information in his mind.

This is an excellent way of conceptualizing the human mind, particularly since it is not easy to get rid of data that was once stored. To keep our minds at optimum functioning, we would be wise to prevent irrelevant material from entering it in the first place. If we would only render ourselves deaf to gossip and to other useless conversation, our minds might well retain information for which we may have some use.

Younger minds may be more efficient simply because the

storage spaces have not been cluttered with useless information. As we advance in years, we allow more and more useless data to enter our minds. No wonder we cannot remember important things.

Be wise. Don't listen to pointless conversation. Don't read worthless material. Since you do not have an infinite amount of money, you budget your money wisely so that you can afford the things you really need. It is even more important to budget your mind wisely.

21.

ARE WE THERE YET?

Vacationing with the kids can be the most enjoyable and/or unenjoyable experience of a lifetime. You can lessen the unenjoyable part if you anticipate the bumps.

You're all set to leave. Everything is packed. You have precise directions to the lake. You have all your fishing gear including hip boots.

You also have three kids in the back seat, and if this is your first trip, you had better be prepared. Soon after the car starts (sometimes even before), the fight begins over who gets to sit by the window. There are only two windows, but there are three kids. You try to explain that during the four-hour drive there will be plenty of time for everyone to have a turn by the window.

"But I want to go first! I'm the oldest!"

"But I called it first. Remember?"

"Nuh uh."

"I did too! Mommy, didn't you hear me call it at breakfast?"

47

Somehow this gets settled, although no one ends up happy with the settlement. About 30 minutes out of the city, Sarah asks, "Are we there yet?"

"I'm tired," Benny says.

"Then lean back and close your eyes."

"I can't lean back. Davy has his big feet on the seat. Anyway, Sarah's been at the window too long. It's my turn."

"I'm hungry," Davy says.

"You can't be hungry. You had a big breakfast just an hour ago."

"I can't help it. I'm hungry anyway."

"You'll just have to wait. When we make our first stop, I'll get you something from the trunk."

Then comes Benny's announcement. "I've got to go to the bathroom."

"I told you all to go to the bathroom before we left. Didn't you hear me?"

"I forgot. I've got to go real bad."

I think you get the idea. You might try and anticipate every eventuality. Leave it to the kids to come up with something you could not have foreseen or could not have done anything about if you had foreseen it, like "I think I'm going to throw up."

Does this mean you shouldn't go on vacation with the kids? Heaven forbid! You will have a lot of fun. And years later when you look at the pictures, you will remember only the good times. (You didn't take pictures of when Davy fell, scraping his knees and nose.)

There is no way to avoid the bumps of a vacation trip. Being forewarned is being forearmed. If you expect these things, it will be easier to take them in stride. And do think about how you will be enjoying the pictures and the memories in years to come.

22

ITS THE STRANGEST THING

To err is human. We all know that. Mistakes are not only excusable, they are even expected. Repeating the same mistake is not expected nor is it excusable. It has been said that insanity consists of doing the same thing and expecting a different result. We expect rational people to be sane.

My father would tell a charming story. In the horse-and-buggy days, a traveler hired a taxi and after telling the driver his destination said, "Be careful to avoid that particular road. There is a huge pit there."

"Just sit back and relax," the driver said. "I've been driving these roads for 35 years."

A bit later the passenger said, "Look, I can see where you're heading. Don't go that way. That road has a huge pit."

"Didn't I tell you not to worry?" the driver said. "I've been traveling these roads for 35 years."

As they approached the road the passenger said, "For heaven's sake! Turn around! You're approaching the pit!" Again the driver reassured him.

Shortly afterward they fell into the pit. As they crawled out from underneath the overturned coach, the driver said, "It's the strangest thing. I've been traveling these roads for 35 years, and whenever I come by here, this is what happens."

You are entitled to make a mistake once. If you didn't put two and two together, you can be forgiven for making the same mistake a second time. But the third time cannot be justified.

Situations within the family tend to recur much more often than with strangers. We may make a comment or do something which offends another family member. Repeating the same mistake a number of times indicates a total lack of consideration. We can hardly expect to be forgiven if we are inconsiderate. On the other hand, avoiding repetition of an irritating behavior will show others that we are sensitive to them. That strengthens the relationship.

23.

A SMOOTHER BLEND

Of all the things that may appear tough at home, blending two families may seem to be the toughest. I'm referring to a second marriage where each spouse has children from a previous marriage. Now they must all live together in the same household. It's even difficult to say that it's not as tough as you think. Rather, let's think of it this way. It can be done. I know of many instances where the two families blended successfully. If they could do it, so can you.

Many powerful forces are at work when two families join. There are a variety of intense emotions, some of which are in stark conflict with others.

I have no intention of writing a marriage manual, and I certainly cannot provide a practical rule of thumb. I just wish to alert you to some things you must consider and suggest a possible source of assistance.

Each parent has had years of bonding with his/her children. Each parent has ideas about raising children and how they should be disciplined. These ideas may be at opposite poles. Each partner may have ideas about money, how much to spend, how much to save, and how much to give the kids. Each parent wishes to be a good stepparent.

We have all heard stories about stepparents. From childhood on we have heard fairy tales about "wicked stepmothers." (Why do we fill young children's minds with fairy tales that are full of hatred and violence?) Children may come into the relationship with the proverbial chip on their shoulders. Stepparents may have corresponding feelings. However, in order to be good stepparents, they may conceal or repress them.

Feelings that are concealed or repressed can cause trouble. You can't fix something which you do not know to exist. The husband and wife should be open with each other about their feelings. All these feelings are normal and can be worked out if they are in the open. There is great risk of parents becoming defensive, and their judgment may be distorted by their feelings.

It is crucial that the bond between the parents be strong and constantly strengthened. The potential for a wedge being driven between the parents is considerable. This may result in damage to everyone.

O.K. What to do? Pre-marriage counseling is important even in a first marriage. It is absolutely crucial in a second marriage. Issues can be identified, and some can be resolved before the marriage. A plan can be drawn about how to deal with the various emotions and sensitivities that are certain to arise. It is much easier to discuss these issues rationally *before* they result in confrontation. Finally, if problems should arise after the marriage, there is recourse to a counselor who is familiar with both partners and the family constellations. This counselor can be more effective than one who has had no previous contact with the couple.

In addition to pre-marriage counseling, it would be helpful if the couple would attend a support group before the marriage. They may hear what types of problems occurred in other blended families. They may learn what types of solutions worked and what didn't. Why make mistakes of your own when you can learn from the mistakes of others? At this point, neither parent is being challenged and there is no need to be defensive. Both parents can use good judgment and come to an understanding about how they will deal with some of the issues that are likely to arise.

A suitable support group may be found through Parents Anonymous or by asking the counselor. The adage that "an ounce of prevention is worth a pound of cure" is nowhere as true as in the blending of two families.

With proper preparation, the process of integration can be facilitated. Many bumps can be avoided.

24.

GETTING THE MESSAGE ACROSS

Sometimes we may do things that seem logical, but which unfortunately have the reverse effect.

Because of the concern about the increase in violence and immoral behavior, parents are having a "V chip" installed in their television sets. This will allow them to regulate which programs their children can watch. Logical? Maybe. Effective? No way.

What would you do if an insect fell into your bowl of soup or coffee? Without a doubt you would spill it out. Why? Because it's disgusting.

You didn't always consider insects to be disgusting. When you were 8 months old, you picked up an insect and were about to put it in your mouth, just as you put everything within reach into your mouth. Your mother saw you and screamed, "Don't do that! Ugh! Dirty! Nasty! Ugh!" This verbal outburst was accompanied by a facial expression of revulsion that was so violent that your revulsion for insects lasts an entire lifetime. You react with disgust 60 years later.

How effective do you think it would have been if mother had not reacted this way but would have said softly, "Now sweetheart, put that bug down. Bugs are not good to eat, you know." Not too effective. Of course, she couldn't have reacted that way. Her personal feeling of revulsion was uncontrollable.

Now just think. Daddy and Mommy do not react to these graphic scenes with revulsion at all. To the contrary. They put in a "V chip" which essentially says, "These scenes are good for Daddy and Mommy, not for you." Instead of turning children away from violence and inappropriate behavior as being loathsome, parents tell them that they really find them interesting, and want to keep these scenes all for themselves.

Perhaps parents do not react with revulsion to these scenes because they don't feel that they are disgusting. Well, how then do you expect your children to feel differently?

Whatever it may be that we want to discourage in our children, we must have a profound feeling and conviction that it is objectionable. When illicit behavior of any type becomes as loathsome to you as eating insects, you are likely to pass on this attitude to your children.

Be careful that you are getting the message across and that you do not send the wrong message.

25.

YOU'RE NOT THAT POWERFUL

There are some people who feel responsible for their family members' moods. One woman said, "If my husband is happy, then I'm happy. I think he is happy with me. If he is in a bad mood, I feel it's my fault and that I'm responsible. I try to do things to make him happy, but it doesn't work."

It may be very egotistical to assume such responsibility. There are umpteen things that could cause a person to be moody. Ascribing the other person's mood to oneself is essentially saying, "There's nothing else in the world that counts for him. The only thing that could possibly affect him is me."

Obviously we should behave in a way that will not aggravate other people. But suppose I happen to be in a mood. Why should I assume that my mood is going to affect everyone else?

We should at all times behave as best we can, with consideration for others. But we cannot make everyone happy. Nor should we assume responsibility if someone appears to be unhappy. How others feel is their prerogative, not our obligation.

26.

IT'S SIMPLE BUT IT'S NOT EASY

Many books have been written on ways to have a harmonious marriage. From the size and number of books on the subject, it would appear that achieving a harmonious marriage is a very complicated task. Many factors must be considered: emotions, attitudes, ambitions, past experiences, methods of effective communication, etc.

All these factors are indeed important. However, there is one brief rule which, in itself, can greatly enhance harmony in the marriage, and which, if neglected, may make all the other efforts of little value. The rule is simple: *Make a sincere commitment to always be **absolutely** truthful with each other.*

An excellent guideline to proper behavior is: *If you think you may at any time have to lie about what you are about to do, then **don't do it!***

Just think how wonderful the relationship would be if husband and wife *never* concealed anything from each other. This would virtually eliminate either spouse doing something of which the partner would disapprove. Many if not most serious problems in marriage are the result of a spouse finding out that the partner has done something that causes him/her displeasure. Inasmuch as admitting the act would result in a negative reaction, spouses would naturally avoid doing things that are objectionable to the partner.

One may promote truth as an ethical virtue. As presented here, truth is a simple, practical method for avoiding domestic strife.

I said that this rule is *simple*. I did not say it was easy. Admitting to a spouse that one has done something wrong is not easy. Always being truthful is not easy. If it were easy, few people would lie. We always look for an easy way to do things.

Concealment can be complicated. One has to fabricate stories to avoid criticism. Then one has to remember the lies one has told and be on guard not to say anything that would reveal the falsehood. Lying may seem easier, but it is complicated. Being truthful may not be easy, but is very simple.

Adopt this rule for a 90-day trial period. If it doesn't work, you can have your money back.

What money? It doesn't cost anything.

See? Not only is this simple rule effective, it is also free.

27

RULES AREN'T MADE TO BE BROKEN

Raising children is tough. In the first *Its Not As Tough As You Think* I suggested that this is one situation where it might even be *tougher* than you think. Even if so, we should still try and find ways to smooth out the bumps.

One of the most difficult problems parents confront is that children today are more defiant than in times past. The 1960s appear to have been a watershed. Respect for authority dwindled to imperceptibility. Why, when I was in grade school we trembled at the thought of being sent to the principal's office. Today's children couldn't care less. Today teachers tremble lest a student eludes the metal detectors and sneaks in with firearms.

All authority has suffered. Court orders are openly defied. Religious leaders find that their flocks do pretty much what they please. Police are on the defensive. Given this cultural attitude, how can we get our children to listen to us?

I think the only chance we have is to show them how it's done. Parents should be a model of deference to authority. Let's think a moment. When is the last time we deferred to authority?

Whether or not you have a "fuzz-buster," violating the speed limit and taking pride in how you got away with it is far from uncommon. One may boast about having gotten away with it while the kids are in the back seat. What do they hear? Dad broke the law and didn't get caught! Wow, that's great! If that's what we teach our kids, how can we expect them to obey our rules? All they will try to do is avoid getting caught.

Suppose a child in the back seat says, "Daddy, how come all those cars are passing you?" You say, "Billy, the speed limit here is 65. I don't care what others do. I obey the law." You've given Billy a powerful lesson in obeying the rules.

There are many other times when we can do this. Let's make it a point to obey rules even if we don't agree with them, even if we could get away with breaking them. Let's model for our kids by deferring to authority even when we disagree with authority. This doesn't guarantee that our children will listen to us, but it does give us a fighting chance.

28.

DREAMS CAN COME TRUE

ost people do not live just for today. Even if life in the present is free of distress, we still dream about the future. We look forward to retirement, although many retirees don't know what to do with themselves all day. Men who were employed full time and who just sit around the house may become annoying rather than enjoyable companions.

While we are in the prime of life it would be wise to begin preparing now for a pleasant retirement. Yes, I know that with more time available you will be able to go on more fishing or skiing trips with friends. I hope that you do. However, we should not rely entirely on activities that may be restricted by conditions that could possibly develop in the golden years of life. We should add on some interests that do not require physical exertion, such as increasing our knowledge, hobbies, interest in music, and yes, crafts.

Even though you are still young, take a stroll through an "arts and crafts" shop. You might find some time to take a course in some craft. Perhaps other family members will take an interest in what you are doing. A new focus of family togetherness may develop.

Arouse your curiosity and interests. The Talmud states that on Judgment Day we will be asked, "Did you appreciate My world?" How will we explain that we did not see the beauty of animal life in the jungles of Africa? How will we defend our failure to see the majesty of the snow-capped mountains of the Canadian Rockies? How is it that so many Jews have not yet visited Israel and so have missed the opportunity to tread on the some soil as did the Patriarchs? The Talmud states that when we see these wondrous places we must recite the blessing praising G-d for His awesome work of Creation. While we may not be able to do this when we are tied down to our jobs, we should plan to do so in the future.

And yes, do not hesitate to think big. In the Bible Joseph dreamed he would one day become a ruler, and he did! Of course, you must keep yourself within reality. You may not become a king, but unless you dream big, you may not even achieve small. Aim for the stars and you may reach the moon. Aim for only the next block and you get nowhere.

People often give me their poetry to read. Just because publishers will not accept it doesn't mean it isn't good, and it is an excellent way of expressing oneself. One of the articles in this book is the result of a poem that a woman wrote. She printed her poems on her desktop printer and made her own little book!

Many people comment, "My life story could make up a book!" Well, if that's how you feel, why don't you write it?

When I was a fledgling student in psychiatry, I felt I had many ideas to share. Every free moment I wrote a page or two. I handed the manuscript to one of my instructors. He returned it with the comment, "Some good ideas, but immature. Give yourself some time. Rewrite it 10 years from now." I waited *fifteen* years, and then wrote my first book on self-esteem, *Like Yourself, and Others Will Too*. You are now holding my 32nd book in your hands. It would have been a mistake to publish the first manuscript I had written 15 years earlier. It would have been a greater mistake not to have written it.

Allow yourself to dream about the future, and do whatever is within your hands to make it happen. You'll be pleasantly surprised to find that the *present* becomes more enjoyable

29

THE BEST THING THAT HAPPENED

I regret that I didn't think of this when my children were young. A friend told me that at the Sabbath meal he asks his children, "What was the best thing that happened to you this week?" The children generally come up with some pleasant experiences.

Sometimes a child will grouch. "Nothing good happened to me. It was a lousy week." To this the parent responds, "O.K. I didn't say the week was good. But of everything that did happen, what was the best thing?" Invariably the child will come up with something. He may think of it as the least worst thing, but even so, it is still the best. That has a positive ring.

Sometimes one of the siblings may chime in with, "Oh yeah? What about when you found the yo-yo you thought you had lost in the park?" This may even lead to a mini-discussion about why he didn't think of that. Furthermore, just as he had forgotten that, maybe there were other good things that he forgot. Maybe it wasn't such a bad week after all. The parent might even remark,

"You know, Joey, you just might be upset by something today. When you're in a bad mood you might not think of good things that happened." This can be a powerful lesson in psychology.

Knowing that he will be asked to report about something good may lead to the child having a positive attitude at the beginning of the week. He may be on the alert for something good.

The phenomenon of "self-fulfilling prophesy" is real. Anticipating something good may result in good things happening, and anticipating bad things may bring them about. Focusing on the positive can be most constructive. It may also imbue the entire household with an upbeat attitude.

30.

PEOPLE PLEASER OR PLEASANT PERSON?

It's great to be liked by everyone. Let's face it. That is not reality. We live in a world where there are senseless prejudices. Some people have criteria which determine whom they will like and whom they won't like.

In *Life's Too Short* I listed some of the behaviors that people use to cope with unwarranted feelings of inferiority. Some people who think of themselves as being unlikable may try to gain acceptance and the affection of others by doing things for them. They become "people pleasers." It's wonderful to do things for others, but acts of kindness should not be motivated by trying to ingratiate oneself. We should do them because that is the right thing to do. If we like ourselves, we will not be desperate to be liked by the whole world. There are about six billion people in the world. If only half of them like me, that gives me three billion who like me. That should be enough for anyone.

We should do our best to live decent lives. This will not guarantee that everyone will appreciate us. If we realize this and have good self-esteem, then we may have the attitude, "If So and so doesn't like me, that's his problem. I'm not responsible for his bad judgment." This does not mean that one should be vain. A person can be humble and yet think of himself as worthy.

Vanity means thinking of oneself as being superior to others. If a person is aware of his G-d-given talents, that should not make him conceited. To the contrary, he should ask himself whether he has fully actualized his potential. If not, then he must do more. Humility is a feeling of not having done all that one can, and this should stimulate a person to greater achievement. We may be humble yet think of ourselves as worthy and as deserving of other's affection.

An individual may have or lack self-esteem. So can a family. A person who has unwarranted feelings of inferiority may resort to various defenses to escape these feelings. Many of these defenses may be self-defeating. The same is true of a family. A family that thinks of itself as being less than other families may also resort to self-defeating behaviors.

Obviously, we should avoid doing things that provoke others. We should not make ourselves unlikable. But if we are kind, just, and considerate, we will be liked by sensible people. If people do not like us even though we live proper and decent lives, they are not sensible. Why should we be upset by the opinions of people who are not sensible?

31.

SMILE AT SOMEONE YOU DON'T LIKE

The Talmud states, "Receive every person with a pleasant countenance" (*Ethics of the Fathers* 1:15). Every person should be greeted with a pleasant demeanor, even someone with whose company you may not be particularly delighted.

In *Visions of the Fathers* I pointed out that the literal translation of the Talmud is, "Receive every person with *an attitude* of a pleasant countenance." In other words, even if you are not thrilled to see this person, act as if you are.

This is not duplicity. It is a *mitzvah* to make another person feel good. This "other person" need not be a friend. It is a *mitzvah* to make anyone feel good.

Furthermore, a smile begets a smile and a frown begets a frown. If you smile at someone and he returns the smile, you too will feel good.

I once ran into a person with whom I had sharp differences and we had parted with mutual ill feeling. When I saw him several years later, I noticed that he was avoiding me. I felt that he was apprehensive, fearing how I might act toward him. I smiled at him, shook his hand, and said, "By now we should both have forgotten our resentments. If we haven't, let's forget them now." What could have been a very unpleasant evening for both of us turned out to be most enjoyable.

We may think that our inner feelings determine our outward actions. This is not necessarily so. Our outward actions may alter our inner feelings. Smile at someone you don't like. You may find that your dislike of him diminishes.

32.

HOW IMPORTANT IS IT?

I learned something of great value.

On one of my trips I was hosted by a scientist friend. He is an internationally acclaimed expert in his field and travels all over the world to lecture.

We were chatting in the evening, when he said, "I'm really glad to be able to be here with you, Abe. I was supposed to be giving an address at two conferences this week, in Brussels and in Paris. But I found out that Arnie has one more football game left in his senior year, and I know he wants me in the stands when he plays."

I was in disbelief. What? Cancel a scheduled appearance at two important international scientific conferences because your kid wants you to watch him play football? Then I realized that this scientist had his priorities straight. His son's performance was top priority. What a way to let a child know he is important!

You say that is a bit extreme? Let's look at the opposite extreme. A young man was arrested in his college town for outlandish behavior and was thought to be mentally ill. The police sergeant said they would drop the charges if the father would come for him and have him admitted to a hospital for psychiatric evaluation. I was contacted and arranged for his admission. However, the father, who was the CEO of a major corporation, was presiding over a stockholders' meeting. The young man had to remain in jail until the meeting was over. My scientist friend would have delegated conducting the meeting to another executive and would have promptly brought his son to the hospital. But then his son wouldn't have behaved in this manner – he knew he was important.

Both cases may appear to be extremes, but they do convey an attitude. How we establish our priorities tells our children just where they stand in the scale of importance. If we show them that they are of primary importance to us, this greatly elevates their self-esteem.

33.

WHAT YOU SEE IS WHAT YOU GET

I t may be a long courtship or a short courtship. The young man and woman may discuss many things that they consider important. They may think that they know everything about the partner that will result in an idyllic marriage.

This is rarely the case. As a rule, one cannot know how the other partner will relate in marriage until the marriage is well under way.

Children's idea of a marriage is primarily developed by their observation of their parents' relationship. A young man who grows up exposed to a father who was controlling very likely assumes this to be the way a husband should act. If the father spent an inordinate amount of time at the office, the son is apt to do the same. If the wife comes from a family that traditionally, maybe even for several generations, gathered at the parental home for Friday-night dinner, she is going to take for granted that this will continue after her marriage. Her married brother and sister eat with the parents every Friday night. Why should she be a renegade? Her husband might prefer some Friday nights alone with his wife. Why doesn't he respect her family tradition?

The possibilities of differences in lifestyle are legion, far too great to enumerate. The point is that young men and women should not assume that they will continue their routine. They should also not think that their partner's resistance to change indicates obstinacy.

There is generally a positive aspect that can be gleaned even from conflict. For example, in the case cited, the young woman should appreciate that her husband wishes to have quality time alone with her. The husband should esteem his wife's respect for tradition. If not for tradition, we would be bereft of much of our value system.

Although love is a powerful force, one should not assume, "I know he/she will change for me." Changes may and will occur. But bear in mind, *a person will change only when he/she wishes to change.* The most serious misconception is that one partner can *make* the other change. Ask the wife of any alcoholic, who had been certain that her copious love would replace the drinking. Or, a far less destructive example, that he would curtail his bowling or fishing with his buddies in order to be with her.

If there were only one statement I could make to a young man or young woman, it would be "What you see is what you get." If you don't like what you see and decide to accept it anyway, that is your decision. Just don't delude yourself into thinking that the part you don't like will disappear.

Marriage should be entered with the understanding that both partners will have to make some adjustments. Pre-marriage counseling is extremely helpful in preventing misunderstandings and arguments. Even then, mutual patience, consideration, and respect are essential in establishing a new relationship.

Approached properly, the blending of two lives can be harmonious. But even at its very best, it's going to take time.

Differences between marriage partners may be thought of as "speed bumps." If you proceed slowly and carefully, you won't feel much roughness.

34.

THAT'S ABSURD

I've seen it many times. A child runs into the corner of the table, bumps his forehead, and cries in pain. Mother rushes to the rescue, embraces the child, and hits the table. "Bad, bad table! You hurt my Sammy!"

PEANUTS reprinted by permission of United Feature Syndicate, Inc.

Why teach the child something so absurd? The table isn't bad. If he believes you he'll run around recklessly again, assuming that the table learned its lesson when you hit and scolded it. Or maybe he'll think that other tables are not as wicked as this one.

How about if you embrace the child and soothe him saying, "Honey, you have to be careful when you run around. If you don't watch out you might bump into things and get hurt." That is constructive teaching.

So often we see people projecting blame on everyone else, totally oblivious to their own role in making things go wrong. You know, everyone else is to blame. The husband, the wife, the kids, the boss, the government, the IRS, etc. It's always someone else's fault. A person will never correct his behavior as long as he can attribute undesirable consequences to someone else.

I wonder whether we might not be responsible for this attitude by doing things like hitting the table instead of cautioning the child to be more careful.

35.

PRANK OR PREDICAMENT

We often enjoy playing pranks on family members. This can be great fun, and is usually well tolerated. But be careful before you pull a prank! Be sure that you don't risk trouble.

Back in the days when people traveled long distances by trains which had sleeping accommodations, Sol was visited by his Uncle Charles. Charles was going to make the long trip home by bus. Sol had a ticket for a Pullman accommodation on the train. Although the ticket was non-transferable, Sol felt that no one would know the difference. His uncle's last name was the same as his. If Charles were asked for identification, no one was likely to notice that the first name was different.

Several days later Sol received a letter. Charles said that the conductor did indeed notice that the first name on the ticket was different than his. He told him that this was fraudulent use of the ticket. He wrote down Charles' address and took Sol's address as well. He said he was going to report this fraudulent use of the ticket. The conductor appeared very angry. Charles said he was sure they were in for trouble. In reality, it was only right that they were caught. What they did was illegal. By not obeying the rules of the company they had committed a crime.

Sol did not bother to finish reading the letter. If he had, he would have read, "The only thing in our favor is that none of this happened." Instead, he ran to the phone and called his lawyer, instructing him to contact the railroad and to offer to pay for the ticket. Fortunately, he did finish the letter before the lawyer had made the call. Charles' prank almost resulted in precipitating a charge of fraud.

This does not mean that one should never pull a prank. That would deprive us of some of the spice of life. But do be careful. Just give some forethought as to possible consequences before indulging in what appears to be harmless fun.

36.

FEELINGS MAY NOT BE WHAT THEY SEEM

"I don't understand why Susan can't stop crying. What's the big deal?"

"Keep your voice down! I won't have that here. You should learn to control your anger."

Sound familiar?

What do you think when you hear belligerent shouting? Someone is obviously angry, right? And when you hear sobbing? Someone feels very hurt, right? Not necessarily.

I did mention this in *It's Not As Tough As You Think*. It is important enough to repeat it in regard to the family, because the more intimate the relationship, the more intense are the feelings. When a child suffers, the parents feel it more acutely than when a more distant relative suffers. If you offend a parent, the guilt is apt to be more intense than if you had offended anyone else. If your spouse disappoints you, the anger you feel may be more penetrating than if it were anyone else. I hardly need point out that the rivalry that can exist between siblings may exceed any other competitive relationship.

There are two points I wish to make about feelings. Firstly, feelings may not be under voluntary control. If a person is provoked, the feeling of anger is almost a natural reflex. A person can certainly be in control of how he *reacts* to provocation. It takes an inordinately high degree of spiritual development not to *feel* anger.

The denial of anger that occurs when a person *represses* anger is not commendable. This is anger that is felt but is quickly repressed, i.e., driven out of awareness. Repressed anger continues to lurk in the deep recesses of the unconscious and can have a harmful effect on a person's emotions and actions. A highly spiritual person may be able to condition himself so that he does not feel angry when provoked. This is beyond the scope of the average person. It therefore makes little sense to say, "You shouldn't feel angry." As a rule, that is not a matter of choice.

A child may go around sulking, obviously angry because of something father or mother said or did to him. Some children are taught that it is disrespectful to feel anger toward a parent, and may be made to feel guilty about their feelings. We may say that it is disrespectful to *act out* anger toward a parent or to hold a grudge against a parent. These can be under one's control. The initial feeling of anger is not, and children should not be expected to rise to the spiritual level where they do not even register anger.

The second point is that anger and pain are next door neighbors, and one can easily enter the wrong house. Further-

81

more, anger can be painful, and very often people in pain are angry about their suffering. Belligerent shouting does not always indicate anger. It may be an expression of pain. Crying may not be due to pain. It may be an expression of anger.

The exchanges of these two feelings may be affected by cultural attitudes. For a man to cry may be thought of as a sign of weakness. In fact, a leading candidate for the presidency had to withdraw from the race because he cried in public! But feelings seek expression. A man who feels like crying may instead act angry. Anger is more macho than crying.

A man may be in a real dilemma. He can't cry because he is a man, but he may be too passive to express anger — and he therefore has no outlet for his feelings. Those who are familiar with this scenario will recognize a frequent response to this problem — the man becomes depressed.

Women, on the other hand, may feel that it is unladylike to be angry. There are some very unkind terms applied to a woman who acts angry. But it is perfectly acceptable for a woman to cry. A woman who is provoked to anger may therefore react by crying.

We can see why the comments at the beginning of this article are inappropriate. If Susan were crying because she was hurt, the crying might be out of proportion to the pain. Crying may relieve some pain, but it is not a satisfactory discharge for anger. The anger may therefore persist unmitigated, and the crying may continue.

Similarly, when the young man is told to stop shouting and

learn to control his anger, the comment is off the mark. Even if he could manage his anger, he may not be able to manage his pain. If the belligerence is an expression of pain, the demand to control the anger is irrelevant.

Inasmuch as feelings among family members tend to run high, it is important that we understand these two points. Failure to understand them can result in unreasonable demands being made. These only add fuel to the fire and may aggravate the unpleasant behavior.

37

IT DOESN'T WORK

I f we cannot really control our children (even infants!), why do we think we can control adults? Yet I frequently see husbands trying to control their wives, wives trying to control their husbands, and children trying to control their parents. Wielding dictatorial control is a mistake

Control and *discipline* are not the same. Control and *direction* are not the same. Husbands and wives should comply with each others' wishes out of affection and consideration, not out of fear. Parents should direct and teach, but they must face the reality that they do not have absolute control. Let's understand why.

Adolescents resist being controlled, and they may even try to control their parents. "I don't want to go to school and you can't make me!" They may manipulate their parents. They may take the car without permission. What are you going to do about it? Report it stolen? They dare you! If you "ground" them, they'll find a way of getting out. Are you going to threaten to kick a 14-year-old out of the house if he doesn't follow rules? He knows

84

you won't do it. He has the upper hand.

It should never get to this stage. What has worked throughout the ages is that parents have taught their children values in a way that makes the children willing to adopt these values as their own. They see that their parents are sincere in their beliefs and are willing to make sacrifices for what they believe. They see that their parents honor and respect their tradition and wish to transmit it to their children. They know that their parents love them and wish to give them what is best for them. When Moses conveyed the word of G-d to the Israelites he told them that the Divine commands are "life and good," and that deviating from them is self-destructive (*Deuteronomy* 30:19). This is what parents should convey to their children.

There is a very simple reason for dispensing with dictatorial control. It doesn't work. Sure, you may intimidate someone into compliance for the short term, and you may delude yourself that you are "in control." It cannot have any durability. Furthermore, it may result in resentment. Children will accept parental ways when the direction is with sincerity and understanding.

Dictatorial control is damaging to self-esteem — to everyone's self-esteem, both those who are doing the controlling and those who are being controlled. Why? Read on.

36.

SELF-ESTEEM IS CONTAGIOUS

Self-esteem is probably the single most important factor in adjusting optimally to life. Parents often ask, "What can we do to build self-esteem in our children?" The answer is twofold. Self-esteem is contagious. Children adopt parental attitudes. If parents are self-confident, children pick that up. If parents are insecure, children are likely to be insecure.

Secondly, there are things that parents can do that are conducive to self-esteem in children. Some excellent ideas are presented in *Building Self-Esteem in Children*, by Patricia Berne. Exerting control over a child depresses his self-esteem. No one feels good about being controlled. Children who have to "follow orders or else" may not have the chance to develop their ability to make judgments. They may grow up incapable of making decisions. On the other hand, if you negotiate with a child, you are showing your confidence in his reasoning ability. You can also teach him how to arrive at a proper judgment.

Let's look at what happens when parents try to control.

Dominating others is often a symptom of low self-esteem. A person with good self-esteem has no need to show that he is the boss. Our greatest world leaders were generally humble people who were pushed into the position of leadership. Exerting dogmatic control betrays a lack of self-esteem in parents, and this may carry over to the children.

Sure, there are times when it may seem appropriate to say, "Do it because I said so!" However, a more wholesome statement is, "I can't explain it to you right now. Do as Daddy/Mommy says. I'll explain it to you later." Not only is the content of this statement healthier, but it is certain to be said in a more conciliatory — albeit "no nonsense" — tone of voice. Incidentally, if you have no explanation, why do you want the child to do it?

Dogmatic control by parents betrays low self-esteem on their part and actually depresses it further. Subjecting children to dictatorial orders depresses the child's self-esteem. Both end up losing. Both may reinforce their ego defenses. The parents may become more domineering, the children may become more defiant, and a vicious cycle is set into motion.

Children need guidance. You may find it hard to believe, but they *want* guidance, and they do not rebel against guidance. But they also want to be respected. Guidance does not have to be delivered in a way that will diminish their sense of self-worth. When we teach them lovingly, we convey our conviction that they will exercise good judgment in following our teachings. That boosts their self-esteem.

39.

NO NEED TO CHOOSE

Our relationships with our parents and children need not be an "either-or." We can often relate well to both.

Many people today find themselves in what has been referred to as the "sandwich generation." Thanks to medical science, we are living longer. Some elderly people may not be capable of total independent living. Their children may find themselves caring for both their parents and children.

In the olden days, several generations lived in the same home. This is not as popular a practice today, but there is much that can be said for it. Grandparents can provide a sense of stability and continuity. Since parents are often at work, grandparents can provide loving care for the grandchildren. Sometimes children may have reflex opposition to their parents, and may more readily accept guidance from their grandparents. Finally, when children see their parents acting with reverence toward *their* parents, this provides potent modeling for them.

There may of course be some inconvenience in having elderly parents in the home. They may not be able to tolerate the sound level of the stereo. They may disapprove of things the younger generation wishes to do. They may require preparation of special foods, and one may have to look after them to make sure that they take their medication. If they are forgetful, their repeating things may be annoying. But after all is said and done, the advantages of grandparents in the home often outweigh these difficulties.

It is possible that conflicts may arise between the needs of the grandparents and the grandchildren, and the sandwich generation may feel themselves in the center of a tug of war. There is no rule of thumb to follow. Each situation must be judged on its own merits.

The friend who promised to take your son to the ball game canceled out at the last minute, and gave you the tickets. You are not able to leave grandpa or grandma alone. Your son is disappointed, and you may feel for him. Don't feel too badly about this. Someday in the future he will know that he may have to sacrifice some comfort for his parents. You will have taught him well.

40.

ORGANIZED IS ORGANIZED

You may have heard that a cluttered desk is a sign of an orderly mind. Don't count on it. Sure, you may be able to put your hands on the paper you are looking for in that pile of stuff on your desk that looks as if it were deposited there by the last hurricane. That does not mean that your mind is orderly. The adage is nothing but a rationalization to defend the chaos one allows to occur.

Maimonides teaches us to avoid extremes. A desk where everything is neatly stacked does not necessarily indicate an orderly mind. It may indicate that one is perfectionistic to a fault. And I do mean to a fault. Perfectionism may be so demanding of one's energies that one would actually be better off with clutter.

As with the office, so with the home. Should clothes, books, and papers be strewn over the living-room floor? Of course not. Do the ashtrays have to be cleaned every day? No. By the way, if you're going to be a perfectionist, begin with your health. You shouldn't have any ashtrays in the first place.

"She's so meticulous a housekeeper that you could eat off her floor." That does not win any brownie points with me. I'm not going to eat off anyone's floor. A clean tablecloth is adequate.

Yes, teach your kids to keep the living room decent, but don't make the living room out of bounds for them. It is a *living room*, isn't it? Similarly, the furniture should be treated with due respect, but it is there to be used. If it is only to be looked at, why spend all that money on it? You could look at it just as well in the store. The things you own are there to serve *you*. You should not be a slave to them.

So steer a reasonable course. Avoid scrupulousness as much as you do sloth.

And just in case you are like me, here's a bit of valuable advice. If you put something away so that you're sure to have it when you need it, be sure to make a note where you put it, and keep the note handy. Otherwise you will discover that you put it away in so safe a place that even *you* don't know where it is.

See? Being too organized can have its drawbacks.

41.

HOLD THAT STRETCH

A spiritual home is a happy home. The Talmud was referring to all physical cravings when it said, "No person ever achieves even half of his desires during his lifetime" (*Koheles Rabbah* 1:34). If the primary motivation in a home is for more wealth or physical pleasures, there will be constant frustration that precludes true happiness.

During the workweek we may not find adequate time for spiritual enhancement. Unfortunately, we are often so preoccupied with work or other activities that we neglect our spirituality. For Orthodox Jews, however, the Sabbath day, when we are free of work and other distractions, is the time when we should tend to our spiritual needs.

Alas! Comes Saturday night, the lights go on and we again drive our cars, talk on the phone (the cellular, no doubt) and operate our computers. What has happened with our spiritual gains of the day? One person stated it succinctly: "My soul had stretched, but it shrank again."

I was at the shoemaker when I heard a customer complain that the stretching of his shoes was ineffective. The shoemaker said, "After I stretch them, you must keep shoe trees in them to maintain their shape. Otherwise they will shrink again."

Yes, our souls may expand on the Sabbath. We review the weekly portion of the Bible, attend services, and study various Talmudical volumes. Unless we do something during the week to maintain the expansion, we may lose gain of the Sabbath.

Even just a few minutes every day spent studying Torah ethics may be enough to hold that stretch. A few extra moments of prayer may preserve the spiritual gains of the Sabbath. When the next Sabbath comes, one begins from an advanced level, and this too is maintained. Gradually one can make enormous spiritual progress.

Let us ask ourselves, "Is my home a happier place now than it was a year ago?" We can make it happier. We must stretch our souls and prevent them from shrinking again.

42.

TURNING THE BABY BLUES INTO TICKLED PINK

T his is a topic to which I devoted almost the entire book *Getting Up When You're Down*. I mention it here because too often remediable conditions are allowed to linger.

"Baby blues" may consist of just a few days when the mother's body undergoes some major changes following the pregnancy. But sometimes the blues persist. Nobody seems to be aware of what's happening, and various manipulations may be tried to help the new mother get over the blues.

What may have happened is that the many changes the mother's body undergoes after she delivers the baby may trigger an imbalance in the body's neurohormones. These are the chemicals that operate within the brain. Normally they are in delicate balance. If this balance is upset, the result may be severe depression (postpartum depression). Proper medical treatment is necessary to restore the delicate balance of the neurohormones. Delaying treatment allows unnecessary suffering to continue. The depressed mother cannot give her infant the proper attention. She may then feel guilty over this, which only aggravates the depression. She may even begin to think, "Maybe I didn't want this baby." This is a very painful feeling.

New mothers can use all the help they can get. It has been said that what a new mother needs is her mother. This is not always possible. But even if she does get adequate rest and help, this may not be enough. A chemical imbalance can cause her to feel depressed.

Early attention to postpartum depression is important. If the "baby blues" do not disappear after the first week, a doctor should be promptly consulted for evaluation. With proper treatment, the mother can have the joy she deserves and be tickled pink with her newborn infant. Hopefully she won't have to cope with our next issue.

43.

WHAT'S IN A NAME?

A name is quite an important thing. After all, it becomes part of our identity and stays with us all through our lives.

But names can be a source of trouble. We don't choose our names. Soon after we are born, our parents choose them for us. Which is O.K. Someone has to do it. Our parents might have individual preferences about what name to give us. As a rule they can come to an understanding. They might give us *both*. That's certainly not uncommon. Of course, they might quibble over which of the two names goes first. They usually settle this amicably.

Enter the in-laws — i.e., the grandparents — and the scene changes radically. Mother's parents may insist that the name come from *their* side of the family. Father's parents are equally adamant that the name come from *their* side. The dispute may escalate into threats. I have already heard grandparents say that if the child does not carry the name they prefer they will never visit again. I've also heard a grandfather say that he intends to put away money for the child's tuition. If they do not give the name he prefers, he will not do that.

This causes a great deal of hullabaloo. The young parents do not wish to aggravate either set of parents. They may begin arguing with each other. The grandparents' obstinacy may create strife between the young parents.

Apparently these grandparents are thinking of themselves rather than of their children. And what about the newborn? This child has to go through all the rigors of growing up. He already owes several hundred million dollars of the national debt. Is it fair to put this additional burden upon him, that he brought about suffering and a rupture within the family?

Let's be sensible. Don't make an issue of the name. Enjoy your children and grandchildren. Don't ruin your own lives and theirs.

44.

TIME HONORED

What I really mean to say is not that something is honored *by* time, but just the reverse: that we honor time.

It is universally accepted that stealing a person's possessions is wrong. It is not as widely recognized that stealing his time may be an even greater offense. A stolen object can be returned. Stolen time, never.

I let my patients know in no uncertain terms that I expect them to be punctual. I may have something important to do, but I will not get started on it because I have an appointment in ten minutes. If the patient is ten minutes late, he has actually deprived me of twenty minutes. Keeping someone waiting for an appointment is a thinly veiled insult. It is essentially telling him that you don't think his time is important.

But what if it is not the patient's fault? There may have been an accident that obstructed traffic. Well, if the patient had to make a flight for an important engagement he would have left early enough because of such a contingency. I have every right to expect him to consider my time as important to me as his flight is to him.

The value of time can be taught in the home, and can begin very early. If we tell a child that we will pick him up at 8:15, then we should not come at 8:30. If we are delayed by something unforeseen, we should do what we would expect from others: Call and tell him that we are delayed.

This does not mean that we run the home with the split second precision of a satellite launching. It does mean that we teach our children respect for time in the only way that is effective: by modeling for them and showing them that we respect *their* time.

45.

PAY FULL ATTENTION

Everything for supper is done. The children are outside play-ing. You have a half-hour before suppertime. There is an important article that the school sent for parents to read. You sit back and begin reading. You're in the midst of this article when your 8-year-old interrupts. "Can I go over to Larry's house to play?" Innocent enough. You might wish to reflect about this. You were planning to have an early supper, and if he goes to Larry's house he'll never be back in time. But on the other hand, why deprive him of friendship?

You may try to answer your son Eddie while your eyes and attention are on the magazine article.

"No, we're having an early supper."

"I'll be back in time."

"You never come back in time. I have to call you three times."

"Why do we have to eat early?"

"Because Daddy has to go away tonight."

Your train of thought on the article has been interrupted and you're upset. This response is unwise for two reasons. (1) You really can't think clearly when your attention is divided. (2) If you answer while still reading the article, the child may conclude that his question does not deserve your full attention. That is not good for self-esteem building.

Unless Eddie's question is an emergency requiring a prompt response — like "Sally locked herself in the closet and can't get out!" — delaying your response a few moments is not lethal. "Honey," you may say, "your question is important and I want to give it my full attention. I'll be finished with this article in just a few minutes, and then I'll be able to listen to you." When you finish the article you say, "O.K., now let me hear your question." Even better, hold him affectionately while listening and explain why he should not go to Larry's house just now. He can go at another time.

Eddie's disappointment at not getting an immediate answer will be tempered by his being told that whatever he is asking for deserves your full attention. And you get to finish your article without interruption.

46.

HOW COME HE'S THE MAYOR?

"Enabling" is a term that often has a negative connotation. In the treatment of addiction, "enablers" are people in the environment of the addict whose tolerance of the addictive behavior allows it to continue. Enablers are to addiction what oxygen is to a flame. They do not *cause* the addiction, but inadvertently may be condoning it. In this sense, enablers may be thought of as bringing out the worst in a person.

However, enablers may be just the opposite. They may enable a person to grow and be productive. An enabler can bring out the *best* in a person. Husbands and wives can be positive enablers for each other.

A mayor and his wife drove into a gas station. The wife mentioned that the gas-station attendant had been one of her suitors. "Aren't you glad you married me instead of him?" the husband asked. "This way you are the wife of the mayor and not of a gas- station attendant."

The wife shook her head. "That's not so," she said. "If I had married him, *he* would have become the mayor."

One of the most moving accounts of positive enabling is related in the Talmud. Rabbi Akiva, perhaps the greatest sage of the Talmud, had been a farmhand of the wealthy Kalba Savua. Akiva was totally illiterate, but Rachel, Kalba Savua's charming daughter, recognized his extraordinary potential and promised to marry him if he would go to the academy to study Torah. Enraged at his daughter for marrying an ignoramus, Kalba Savua disowned her. The young couple lived in abject poverty until Akiva left for the academy.

Akiva's brilliant mind soon grasped the basics of Torah study, and he went on to dazzling heights. After 12 years he returned home with a huge entourage of disciples. As he approached his house, he heard a neighbor say to Rachel, "How long are you going to continue a widow-like existence, since your husband has deserted you?" Rachel answered, "Akiva has not deserted me. He is studying Torah, and if he would listen to me, he would stay there for 12 more years." Upon hearing this, Rabbi Akiva turned around and went back to the academy for another 12 years.

After the 24 years, Rabbi Akiva returned with a following of many thousands of disciples. Rachel came to greet him, and the students, not knowing who she was, blocked her access to their master. Rabbi Akiva then spoke his immortal words. "All that I know of Torah, and all that you know, is all due to her."

Positive enabling is not always appreciated. I know of instances where a wife worked to enable her husband to become a doctor or lawyer. Because of poor self-esteem, these professionals were unable to accept that they owed their success to their wives. Instead of acknowledgement and gratitude, they developed resentment against the wife who had enabled them to succeed.

Husbands and wives should be positive enablers and take pride in their partners' success. As they maximize their potential, they should be grateful for the support and stimulus they were given. The words of Rabbi Akiva should reverberate in the ears of all spouses, as they acknowledge the contributions of their partners.

47.

AN OUNCE OF PREVENTION

Many of the "bumps" at home are due to problems presented by raising children: refusal to listen to parents; not getting schoolwork done; trouble getting along with teachers and/or friends, etc. It may seem somewhat surprising that there is so much difficulty. We have some excellent guidelines on how to relate to children in order to avoid these problems. There is the series of books by Dr. Chaim Ginott; an excellent book, *How To Talk So Kids Will Listen & Listen So Kids Will Talk*; and *Positive Parenting*, to name just a few. However, parents who have read these books say that while the advice makes sense, they find it difficult to implement.

I believe the problem was best summed up by Rabbi Samson Raphael Hirsch. A father of several young children consulted Rabbi Hirsch for advice on how to be a good parent. Rabbi Hirsch responded, "You've come much too late."

Most parents have their first recourse to the books on parenting when they begin to experience problems managing their children. Rabbi Hirsch was right. By then it may be far too late. Firstly, parents have already developed ways in which they are relating to their children, and it is not easy to change one's pattern. Secondly, if the parents do change, the children may be confused by the changes. Thirdly, by this time the parents are experiencing the other stresses of family life. There may be financial worries, job insecurity, and perhaps just the stress of having to manage the house. Finally, father and mother might not see eye to eye on methods of parenting. These are not the optimal conditions for learning good parenting techniques.

The time to learn how to best raise children is *before* one is married. None of the above stresses are present, and prospective parents can plan and adopt what they feel to be effective methods of parenting. Before the first child is born, husband and wife can come to an agreement on how they are going to relate to their children, and they will have a unified approach.

This could be accomplished by courses of instruction on parenting in the last two years of high school. Young men and women could discuss the various confrontations that occur between parents and children. Furthermore, they are at an age where their own experience with *their parents* is not ancient history. They can draw upon these experiences and see how they might have more efficient responses. In addition, they may recognize that although they were displeased with their parents' responses to them, these were nevertheless done with good intentions. They may therefore overcome some resentment they have been harboring as a result of having misunderstood their parents.

One might think that children who were unhappy with how their parents related to them would not repeat this pattern with *their* children. They often say, "When I have children I'll never treat them the way my parents treated me." As logical as this may sound, the facts are otherwise. Children who have experienced negative parenting generally repeat the negative behavior with their children. The perpetuation of negative parenting might well be interrupted if young men and women had adequate instruction on parenting before they become parents.

This is not difficult to accomplish. There are competent instructors who could teach courses in parenting in high schools. I am certain that we will find a high interest among students for such courses. Parents and educators should join forces to implement such programs. The benefits to all are incalculable.

48.

WHOM CAN WE BLAME?

Sometimes I think that there are *four* essentials to life rather than three: 1) food and water; 2) clothing; 3) shelter; and 4) *someone to blame*. Blaming is very popular and convenient. It seems that if you can blame your problems on someone, you don't have to do anything about them. "I'm this way because my wife nags me." The implication is, "Call my wife, Doctor, and get her to change and I'll be fine." Not true. The person may not want to make changes in himself, so he blames his wife.

Some psychologists seem to convey the message that all problems are the result of poor parenting. Obviously, how we act toward our children is important. We must do our utmost to parent wisely. However, when clients blame their parents for whatever predicament they are in, I say to them, "Even if you are what your parents made you, it's your own fault if you stay that way."

Let's look at the Scriptures. The very first narrative tells about how Adam and Eve went wrong. Can this be blamed on their parents' mistakes? Perhaps the reason the Scripture begins with this episode is precisely to tell us that we should not necessarily attribute children's misbehavior to parental dereliction.

Blaming others accomplishes nothing. On the other hand, blaming oneself may not be helpful either. Whether we are parent or child, husband or wife, brother or sister, let's stop blaming and see what we can do to improve things.

49.

FINE TUNING

 C ouples usually take care not to hurt each other. However, they may inadvertently do so because each may be unaware of the partner's sensitivities.

Until we really get to know a person, we may assume that his/her sensitivities are similar to our own. We avoid doing things that we would consider offensive. We may not realize that there are very likely some differences in our sensitivities. Things that we would dismiss or accept as good humor might be perceived totally different by one's spouse. This is especially true early in the marriage, when husband and wife have not yet come to know each other well.

My friend's wife told me the following:

Her husband had made a few "kidding" remarks, totally unaware that he had touched a raw nerve. She brought this to his attention. She told him that although he may not have meant it that way, she felt he was belittling her.

Her husband apologized. He said he was truly sorry that he

110

had hurt her feelings. In no way had he intended anything other than what he had thought was an innocent "kibitz." These are the kinds of remarks that a loving husband and wife may make to each other. My mother used to quote a proverb, "Ver es liebt zich, neckt zich." This means that people who love each other kibitz each other.

The wife told me that her husband enjoyed chocolate. When she offered him a piece of chocolate, he said, "I decided not to eat chocolate for a while. I had hurt you because I wasn't thinking about your sensitivity. If I had, I wouldn't have made those remarks. When I pass up chocolate, it will remind me that I have to be more thoughtful of your sensitivities."

A few weeks later she again offered him a piece of chocolate. He said, "Not yet, honey. I still want to be reminded."

He could have bought his wife a little gift as a symbol of his remorse. Perhaps what he did was even more meaningful. It was an indication that he indeed cared about her feelings, and that he would be cautious not to hurt her.

50.

PUT RESPONSIBILITY IN ITS PLACE

Many of us have attended Bar Mitzvahs. What is the most significant part of the event? The young man's recitation of the liturgy? His reading of the Scripture? His address? The party that follows? The correct answer is: none of the above. The most significant part is an oft-overlooked declaration recited by his father: "Thank You, G-d, for relieving me of the responsibility for this boy's behavior."

According to Jewish law, a young boy is a minor until the age of 13. He then becomes an adult, fully responsible for his actions. Prior to age 13, the father bears the responsibility. Once he reaches the age of majority, the father is divested of this responsibility, and it rests totally with the young man.

Since we must abide by the prevailing law of the land, a father may be held legally responsible for his child's behavior until a later age. But the point to remember is that *when a person becomes responsible for his own behavior, no one else should bear that responsibility.*

The principle in this is that responsibility rests with one person, not with two. If you assume responsibility for someone else's behavior, you are permitting him to shed his share of the responsibility. To the degree that you hold yourself responsible for another's behavior, to that degree he will consider himself free of that responsibility.

This principle can have broad application in families. A striking example of this is when someone in the family gets into serious debt as a result of gambling. Well-meaning family members may try to extricate the person by paying off his debts. Or, if someone persists in passing worthless checks, family members may rush in to prevent the person from being charged with a crime. What they do not realize is that by assuming the responsibility for this person's errant behavior, they are freeing him of that responsibility. Invariably, that person will continue doing what he had been doing, in spite of his promises to the contrary. Why? Because he has been shown in the most emphatic way that other people and not he are responsible for his behavior.

Talk about things being tough in the family. Nothing can be as tough as the consequences of assuming the responsibility for other people's behavior once they have reached the age of legal majority.

Family members, especially parents, may think that to allow the person to suffer the consequences of his behavior is too tough. What they do not realize is that by relieving him of that responsibility they are actually making things *tougher* for him and for the rest of the family as well.

A number of years ago I wrote a book, *Caution: Kindness Can Be Dangerous to the Alcoholic*, in which I elaborated on this concept as it applies to the family of the alcoholic. They often extricate the alcoholic from the difficulties brought about by the drinking. They may think they are being kind, but it is a very dangerous kindness.

The same holds true for all other human behavior. We should certainly try to help other people. However, we should realize that relieving them of the responsibility that they should bear is not in the least bit helpful.

51.

ON THE OUTS WITH THE IN-LAWS

I know that someone might think, "What nerve! Including a chapter titled 'On the Outs With the In-Laws' in a book entitled *It's Not as Tough as You Think*. If he knew *my* in-laws, he would not have done that."

O.K. You may be having some difficulty with your in-laws. I never said that it is not tough. Rather, it doesn't have to be *all* that tough. There is always a way to mitigate even the most difficult relationship.

Obviously, we cannot cover all the possible situations. But let's take just one true-to-life case and see how it could have been eased a bit.

Arthur and Belle had been married for seven years and had two children. When they came for counseling they were on the verge of separating.

Belle's father was a wealthy businessman. Although he was a domineering person, he was fanatically devoted to his children. He wanted his children to have the best of everything. Belle loved and worshiped her father.

Belle's father was disappointed when she became engaged to Arthur. He was a scholarly type who loved to teach. Belle's father knew that Arthur could never earn enough as a teacher to provide for his daughter in the way she was accustomed. Belle's two brothers were business oriented and shared in the family business. Arthur didn't fit. Belle's father thought him to be a nerd, and Arthur felt this very keenly. Furthermore, since Belle was so enamored of her father, wouldn't she share his opinion of Arthur?

Belle's father periodically gave her money so that she could have the better things in life. Arthur wished that Belle would have said, "Thank you, Dad. But I married Arthur knowing he would never be rich. An occasional present is wonderful, but we can really get along fine on our earnings." But Belle did not say that. She felt her father would take that as an offense.

At one family gathering the father announced they were going to celebrate their 35th wedding anniversary by going on a cruise. All the family was to go. He then turned to Arthur and said, "Don't worry. I'll take care of your bill." Arthur felt the blood rush to his head. He had been humiliated in front of the family. He had been told that while everyone else could carry his own weight, he would be given a ticket as alms. He really wanted to throw the cruise in his father-in-law's face, but said nothing. Nor did Belle say anything.

On the way home, Arthur exploded. He told Belle that by her silence she had been an accessory to his humiliation. He recited a long list of times when his father-in-law had belittled him and Belle had never come to his rescue. "You're more married to your father than you are to me. You're loyalty is to him, not to me. You're always concerned about how he feels, but you don't care how I feel. Every time he puts me down, you just stand there and agree with him. Why don't you go back to him?"

Belle had no idea of what Arthur was talking about. Her father was just trying to help them out. He never gave them orders. He never meddled in their marriage. She had never felt that he was putting Arthur down. Why did he feel humiliated?

Belle's admiration of her father precluded an awareness that perhaps what her father was doing was not in their best interest. Arthur had swallowed what he had considered "put downs" and had never shared his feelings with Belle. Arthur could have been more assertive and said to his father-in-law, "Dad. I know you love us and want to give us everything you can. Belle and I had discussed our different economic backgrounds before we were married, and she knew we would never be rich. She married me with her eyes wide open. We'll do O.K. on our earnings. Please understand."

Arthur's failure to take this stand and his expectation that Belle would do battle for him could only reinforce his father-in-law's opinion that he was not much of a man.

Had Arthur shared his feelings with Belle and been more assertive, Belle would very likely have supported him, although she could not take the initiative. If this issue had been clarified

117

when Arthur first felt it early in the marriage, there would not have been an accumulation of seven years of resentment toward Belle and her father.

Fortunately, this marriage was saved by competent counseling. By this time it had indeed become a very "tough" situation. If the problem had been dealt with earlier, it would not have escalated to this severity.

So, even some in-law problems do not have to be as tough as they are allowed to become. They should be dealt with at the earliest possible time. There may not be a need for more than brief counseling to set things straight.

52.

BE FAIR, DON'T COMPARE

I s raising children tough? You bet! But it does not have to be as tough as you think.

The verse in *Proverbs* (22:6) — "Train the child according to his nature; when he grows older he will not deviate from it" — has been given various interpretations. One of them is: Every child has a particular natural makeup. If you train the child in a way that is compatible with his natural makeup, you will succeed. If you try to override his natural makeup and direct him in ways that are not natural to him, you will fail in your endeavors. As he grows older he will revert to his natural way.

We know how foolish it is to force a left-handed child to become right-handed. It is similarly wrong to try and mold a child in a way that is contrary to his inborn inclinations.

Each child is unique. It is a mistake to compare them. Some parents have had difficulties with a child because he/she is not as scholarly as a sibling. One child may be academically talented, but cannot carry a tune or hammer a nail. Another child may have manual dexterity or be musically talented but is not a scholar. Parents sometimes set values on academic achievement, and children who do not excel in their studies may not have a sense of worthiness.

Obviously, it is necessary for children to know fundamental also reading, writing, and arithmetic. In my home, fundamentals also include knowledge of Hebrew and all Jewish law and practice. Beyond this, parents should encourage the child to develop his talents. One child may be business minded at an early age. Another may be athletic. Another may be a nature lover. Another may be mechanically inclined, and can tinker with motors all day.

Children should be encouraged to actualize their particular potentials. Of course, this means that parents must get to know their children more thoroughly. The child who can take apart and reassemble an automobile engine has every right to be as appreciated as the one who always makes the honor roll.

It is important that children know that they are appreciated for what they are rather than for trying to be what someone else wants them to be.

53.

NO NEED TO FEEL GUILTY

Guilt can be a healthy and constructive feeling when it is the result of a wrongful act. It stimulates us to make amends and to avoid repeating the act. However, excessive or unwarranted guilt can be problematic. It not only depresses a person, but can also impact negatively on others.

When I worked in the intensive-care unit, I would sometimes observe the behavior of the family of someone who had suffered a heart attack. At times the wife would feel guilty, thinking that perhaps she had made excessive demands on her husband which caused him much stress. Or perhaps she had not watched his diet carefully and allowed him foods that raised his cholesterol. The children may have felt that they had too often pressured their father for money, or had aggravated him by disobedience.

Sometimes the family's guilt would cause them to be over solicitous. They would apologize profusely, which conveyed the feeling that they wanted to ask the patient to forgive them before

121

he died. In one case a brother who had not spoken with the patient for 15 years came to make amends. There was no question that the message was, "I want to make peace with you before you die." Such messages may dangerously increase the patient's anxiety.

At other times the family appeared to be denying the severity of the illness. "Don't worry. With modern treatment, you'll be up and about in no time." The patient's feeling was, "Good G-d! They're not even going to give me a chance to recuperate."

I had read a report by doctors who were treating their heart attack patients with *dauerschlaf* (extended sleep). They would sedate the patient heavily, allowing him to be awake for only brief periods to eat. They claimed excellent results, attributing this to the elimination of anxiety during the first few days.

I suggested another approach. Let the patient stay awake and put *the family* to sleep for a week. That might be an even more effective way of eliminating anxiety.

We should never put excess demands on anyone. Let's try to avoid causing aggravation. That way, if illness occurs, there will be no need to feel guilty.

54.

DO IT YOURSELF?

While many things are not as tough as you think, some things are tougher. The problem is, they may appear deceptively simple.

Remember the process for making paper out of rags? You go through a number of steps, then throw out the concoction and go buy paper. This often happens when you do it yourself.

It's quite safe to hang a picture or even to replace the washer on a leaky faucet. But if it gets a bit more complicated than that, be very cautious. You may wish to save money by doing your own plumbing repair. If you can do it, you will save $50. If you break a pipe and flood the basement, you may end up calling the emergency service late at night or on a Sunday (when else do you have the time to do it?). The rates are double and the job much greater, and you are out over $300.

I once did a simple rewiring of an electric appliance. I shorted the circuit and blew a fuse. Unfortunately, I could not find which fuse was the culprit. It took the electrician less than a minute from when he entered the house to correct the problem. How much? $45.

You've heard that "our eyes are bigger than our stomachs." The same is true of do-it-yourself projects. Making that bookcase by yourself looks so thrilling! You get the tools, the lumber, the nails, etc. You begin the work with enthusiasm. It's strange how the enthusiasm tends to fade once you get started. Two weeks later, there is still a pile of lumber, sawdust, and shavings. You'll get back to it when you have time, right?

Save yourself a headache. Leave the do-it-yourself to people who really know how to do it themselves.

55.

PILLS CAN'T SOLVE EVERY PROBLEM

Some people think that there is a pill for everything. If they are in any way upset or have some trouble sleeping, they reach for a pill. If they are having difficulty with a child's behavior, they expect the doctor to prescribe a medication. Other people are violently opposed to taking any medication that can affect behavior. They believe that all behavior problems should be brought under control by some psychological approach, whether therapy or discipline.

As is most often the case, extreme positions are usually wrong. We now know that there are a number of psychological problems that are best treated with medication. Psychotherapy together with medication may be helpful, but psychotherapy alone may not be effective for those conditions where a chemical imbalance underlies the problem. Withholding medication when it can relieve these conditions is a mistake.

On the other hand, one should not expect medication to resolve everything. Parents who are having difficulty with a child's behavior may pressure their doctor to prescribe Ritalin. This medication may indeed be helpful in some cases of Attention Deficit Disorder (ADD). However, this diagnosis should be made only by someone with competence in children's problems. Some types of children's behavior problems may require therapy for the child and counseling for the parents. It seems easier to try and solve the problem with a pill.

There are also some types of behavior that worry parents, and they may accept advice from friends: "Just leave it alone. It's a phase. He'll outgrow it." This may be true, but it is not always so. When a professional with competence in child psychology tells you this, you can rely on it. However, you should not overlook a condition which may require therapy in the hope that it will go away by itself. If it does not, then you have lost valuable time.

If a child's behavior interferes with his education or with his socializing, allowing it to go unattended may aggravate the problem considerably. Children who fall behind in school or who have difficulty in relating to their peers may conclude that they are stupid or unlikable. This attitude may depress their self-esteem, resulting in a loss of self-confidence. The latter may lead to further impairment in schoolwork and social withdrawal, setting up a vicious cycle. Early evaluation of a problem can prevent unnecessary suffering for both the child and parents.

This is equally valid for grown-ups. Life is full of stresses, and there are unfortunate occurrences that bring about sadness. Not all sadness constitutes depression. Grief upon the loss of a loved one is not an illness. Anxiety because one has lost one's job is not a disease. Some conditions of distress should be managed by counseling or psychotherapy. Others should be relieved by support from family and friends.

There are some conditions which may closely resemble normal grief or anxiety, but which are in fact due to an imbalance of the substances in the body that regulate emotion. To "tough out" these conditions is a mistake. Furthermore, it is possible that the grief over a loss or the anxiety over a setback may actually bring about a disturbance in body chemistry.

I have come across people who obstinately refuse to take appropriate medications. They think that taking an antidepressant means that they are mentally ill. They fear being labeled as "crazy." In many cases, their symptoms may progress to very serious proportions.

One does not consult a neurologist at the first signs of a headache. However, if the usual headache remedies are ineffective and the pain persists, one consults a physician. Emotional symptoms should be dealt with similarly. One need not consult a psychiatrist at the first sign of emotional distress. However, if it persists more than a few days or interferes with one's normal function, it is wise to consult a physician

While antidepressant drugs are generally not addictive, many commonly used tranquilizers can result in addiction if a person becomes dependent on them. Narcotics should be used only for short-term management of pain, and the same holds true for tranquilizers used for relief of emotional discomfort. Check with your doctor whether a medication is potentially addictive. If it is, take caution. A good rule of thumb is that if you need more than one refill, consult your physician about whether you should continue its use. Treatment of addiction to tranquilizers may actually be more difficult than treatment for use of heroin or cocaine!

It has been said that a doctor who treats himself has a fool for a doctor and a fool for a patient. This is equally true of a layperson. If anxiety, sadness, or sleeplessness persists longer than expected, and if home remedies do not work, be wise. Consult someone who can evaluate the problem.

56

IF IT'S LOVE, WHY IS IT SO TOUGH?

B y definition, this is one of the tough "bumps" in life. Indeed, it may be the toughest bump. The term refers to the firm attitude family members must take when one of the family is engaged in self-destructive behavior and refuses to do anything about it. In fact, the person may fight off anyone who tries to help. This may be compared to trying to save a drowning person who, in his panic, may fight off the rescuer. In order to save the person from drowning, the rescuer may have to deliver a harsh blow to the head to render the person unconscious. He can then pull him out of the water. This "assault" is hardly cruel; it is lifesaving.

The most common examples of this are the alcoholic, the drug addict, and the compulsive gambler. These people may be destroying themselves and inflicting serious damage on other family members. Unless these individuals experience a severe crisis, they are likely to continue their destructive behavior. Anything the family does out of "kindness" to prevent the crisis is actually detrimental to the addict. Out of love for the person, the family must allow the addict to feel the consequences of the destructive behavior. This attitude is "tough love."

There is nothing more difficult for family members than to practice tough love. Imagine parents whose son has been arrested because of a drug related crime who are told to keep hands off. Do *not* get him a lawyer. Do *not* bail him out. The parents must enforce the rule that their home is off limits to anyone who uses drugs. If the child continues to use drugs, he must live elsewhere. Can you imagine the agony of parents who must evict their own child and change the locks on the doors?

The compulsive gambler may appeal to family members to "lend" him the money to pay his debts because the "mob" has threatened to kill him. How can they refuse his plea? Yet they must. If he steals from them they must press charges. If he commits credit card fraud or passes bad checks they must not cover up for him. This is probably the most painful thing that any parent can ever experience.

If "tough love" is indeed so painful, how can it be included in a book entitled *It's Not As Tough As You Think?*

Yes, it is very tough. However, parents seem to have no problem in taking their infant to the doctor for immunization. "Protecting" the baby from the misery of pain and subsequent fever by avoiding immunization is hardly kind. The child is then vulnerable to crippling diseases. A loving parent does what is for the child's benefit even though it means inflicting pain.

Parents and family members must learn enough about the course of untreated addiction and its dreadful consequences. They must come to understand that preventing the addict from suffering the consequences of his behavior is like skipping the immunization.

Family members of an addict must get proper guidance. The addict is unable to listen. The family must listen. Counselors who are competent in addiction treatment can provide such guidance. Support groups such as the Al-Anon, Nar-Anon, and Gam-Anon family groups are invaluable sources of information and help. People who have "been there" know what works and what does not work.

It is no doubt tough for a mother to see her baby being hurt by the injection. It is not *as tough* because she understands that this is lifesaving. "Tough love" may be rendered a bit less tough by learning more about addiction and getting the proper guidance.

57.

IT WON'T GO AWAY ON ITS OWN

Just as the distress of implementing "tough love" can be tempered somewhat by proper counseling and support, so can the distress of abuse be somewhat mitigated if the proper steps are taken.

Abuse within the family can be classified into three types: child abuse, elderly abuse, and spouse abuse. Generally, the only one who can seek help is the spouse. Children and the elderly are often incapable of seeking help. In these situations, identification of the problem and initiation of help must come from without.

Obviously, we cannot even begin to elaborate on these problems here. We must remember that no human being should ever be subjected to abuse, whether physical or emotional. It is important to know that if abuse does exist, it is not going to go away on its own. Some type of help is necessary.

In cases of spouse abuse, the abused partners may not seek help. They may resign themselves to their plight. They may think that nothing can be done. They often think that the hardships that may ensue from seeking help may be worse than the abuse. While there may not be any simple solutions, counseling *from someone experienced and competent in abuse problems* may help the person cope more effectively.

Children or the elderly who are abused are often at the mercy of the abuser and may not be able to seek help. The abuse may come to the attention of other family members, friends, physicians, teachers, or the clergy. Sometimes the law requires the reporting of abuse to the proper authorities. In any case, people who are interested in helping a victim of abuse should avail themselves of proper guidance so that they can take constructive steps. The staff of Family & Children's Services are generally competent to evaluate a problem and provide guidance. Without proper guidance, well-meaning people who have good intentions may do the wrong thing.

As with the "tough love" that is necessary in relating to the recalcitrant addict, the "toughness" of abuse situations can be mitigated by a better understanding of the problem and competent advice. It may still be tough, but then it may not be as tough as you think.

58.

MARRIAGE IS NOT A HOSPITAL

There are some people who are chronically unhappy. They may have a very pessimistic outlook. In psychology there is a term "anhedonia" which means that a person is incapable of feeling pleasure.

Men or women who are single may feel that getting married will make them happy. Most often they find that they are no happier after they are married. They may then blame the marriage for their unhappiness and may divorce.

Marriage does provide love and companionship. People feel whole when they have a family. However, marriage should not be expected to solve a person's emotional problems.

It is always easy to attribute the way one feels to some cause, although the two may not be related. One young man tried to solve his unhappiness by marrying. He then attributed his persisting unhappiness to the fear that he might not be able to have children. When his wife conceived he thought his unhappiness was due to his worry whether the child would be born healthy.

The child was indeed healthy, but the colic and teething gave him reasons to explain his mood. This was repeated with the next two children. Then he was worried whether he would have enough money for their education. When he reached age 55, his children were married and independent. He was financially secure. He bought a beautiful new home. However, he was still unhappy. He then concluded that it was his wife who was the cause of his unhappiness, and they divorced. After the divorce he was even more unhappy, but was too proud to reunite with his wife.

The point is that if you're a person who is never happy, seek some professional counseling. Don't try to treat your depressed mood by getting married. Marriage is not a hospital.

59.

PEACE ACCORD

There is nothing more conducive to a happy family life and the healthy emotional development of children than a home in which there is true peace. The Talmud gives *shalom bayis* (peace in the home) the top priority. But peace must be *true* peace. And, it should also be a peace of truth.

The Talmud relates that the wife of one of the sages was a difficult woman who would do the opposite of what was requested of her. Her son would not tell her what his father had requested for dinner but would suggest something totally different. She would then cook the opposite, which often turned out to be what her husband had really wanted.

When the sage discovered his son's tactic, he expressed his appreciation, but told him that even for a good purpose, one may not tell a lie. He indeed wished to restore a better climate in the home, but not at the price of deviating from the truth.

It was this sage who said, "A person should never cause himself to be feared in the home." He advocated a peace based on truth, as well as a true peace.

What do I mean by true peace? Let me explain what a "non-true" peace is.

A visitor to Communist Russia was taken to the zoo by an official guide. "See," the guide said, "here in Russia we have already reached the Messianic era. Look at that cage. A lion and a lamb are living peacefully in the same cage."

The visitor was deeply impressed. When he came to a friend's home that evening he expressed his amazement. After looking around to make sure no one was within earshot, the friend whispered, "What the guide did not tell you is that they give the lion a fresh lamb every day."

There is a kind of "peace" that can be achieved at the cost of great sacrifice. If the husband-father rules the house with tyranny and everyone is afraid to say anything that might upset him, there is indeed a kind of "peace" in the home, but it is not the kind that leads to anyone being happy.

True peace exists where there is mutual love and respect. Husband and wife should respect each other. The Talmud says, "A husband should love his wife as much as he loves himself, and should respect her *even more* than he respects himself" (*Yevamos* 62b). It is interesting that in codifying the laws, Maimonides quotes the Talmud but reverses the order and puts respect *before* love. Why? Because affection is a feeling which develops over time. Giving respect is a behavior which should begin from day one.

True love can exist only where there is respect. In absence of respect there is no love. What is thought to be love is only passion or desire. These are selfish feelings which are not conducive to peace in the family. The Scripture states that love can render a person oblivious to all defects (*Proverbs* 10:12). Only true love can allow a person to overlook the shortcomings of the beloved. Passion does not do this on a lasting basis.

True love results in true peace and happiness. Selfish passion can result only in a quiet house. Everyone is silent for fear of upsetting someone. This is not peace.

Maimonides was so right. First you must respect. Then you can love.

Respect should prevail among all family members. It goes without saying that children should respect their parents. There is also a kind of respect which parents should have for their children. For example, parents should respect a child's privacy wherever possible. This gives the child a feeling of dignity and worthiness, so essential for self-esteem. Parents should also respect a child's feelings. Children may have to be helped to channel their feelings into appropriate behavior, but parents should not deny the children's rights to feelings. Let's discuss this a bit further.

60.

LITTLE PEOPLE, BIG EMOTIONS

hildren can be the source of many "bumps" for their parents. The severity of these bumps can be lessened or increased, depending on how the parent reacts.

Sally is a sixth grader who comes home from school, slams the front door, and throws her books on the floor. She runs to her room, again slamming the door.

This is indeed unacceptable behavior. Mother might march into Sally's room and say, "Young lady, this kind of behavior is not tolerated in this house." But what about Sally's feelings? She was obviously hurt by someone. Don't her feelings count? And why enter her room without knocking? Surely mother would object if Sally walked into *her* room without knocking.

In *Positive Parenting* I suggested an approach which would assert the mother's authority while acknowledging the child's feelings. This approach also allows the child to accept guidance from a parent who is empathic rather than dictatorial. Acknowledging feelings does not mean that the parent approves of the child's behavior. However, children can be taught to behave properly only if parents teach them how they should handle feelings. Denying their right to these feelings makes it impossible to teach them proper behavior.

Believe it or not, sometimes a child is right and the parent is wrong. One parent said, "I don't think I should apologize to my child, even if I was wrong. That would undermine my authority." Pray tell me, where should children learn that one should apologize if their parents do not model for them? Apologizing to a child does *not* undermine parental authority. It does acknowledge the child as a person, and gives him self-esteem. In addition, it shows the child that the parent is in fact human. Maybe children would relate much better to their parents if they were not coerced into considering them infallible. They might even understand why parents need to have an evening off, or go away for a few days by themselves.

Children are little people, but they are people, and should be treated as such.

61.

OLD DOESN'T MEAN OBSOLETE

all me whatever you wish. Ultra-conservative, reactionary, male chauvinist. I'm still going to tell you what I think.

We are often influenced by our environment in ways we may not be aware of. For example, we have high regard for things that are new. You may have spent a great deal of money for a piece of equipment, yet when a new model comes out, there is a desire to get it even if it is not that much different than the old one. The '60s were a watershed. Young people advocated dumping everything that was old just because it was old. Some of that attitude may still be with us. A serious mistake.

The old, traditional lifestyle was that the husband worked to support the family, and the wife took care of the home and the children. Enter the women's liberation movement. Women could become lawyers, doctors, and business executives. Nothing wrong with that for the woman who chooses a career. However, the opening of this frontier was not always seen as providing a *choice*. Some women considered it a duty or obligation. To remain at home and look after the children was an obsolete practice, characteristic of the days when women were repressed. To be "only a mother and housewife" was tantamount to abandoning the cause.

Some women who would have wished to be housewives and mothers felt compelled to pursue a career, and they sacrificed their maternal drives. Some did not wish to surrender their role as mothers, yet also wished to fulfill what they felt was expected of them, i.e., to become a career person. They therefore tried to do both. They wished to prove themselves equal to their male counterparts, and also wished to be good mothers. For some, such demands were excessive and took a severe emotional toll.

It is sometimes necessary for a woman to work. Some women may wish to pursue a career. However, the woman who chooses to be a housewife and mother has every reason to feel proud and fulfilled. Providing a loving home and emotional as well as physical nurture for the children should be acknowledged as an important contribution to the world. It is every bit as great an achievement as being a professional or an executive.

142

62.

WHAT ELSE IS THERE?

Nancy Reagan launched her drug prevention campaign with the slogan "Just Say 'No' to Drugs." Some psychologists and social workers interviewed youngsters for their reaction to this. They reported that a number of 13- and 14-year-olds responded, "Why say 'No'? What else is there?"

I was shocked by this report. Why should young people who are just beginning to live feel that they have nothing to look forward to? Why should they be willing to jeopardize their lives and expose their brains to dangerous chemicals?

The fact remains, many young people do feel this way. But why?

Some young people may have profound feelings of inferiority and inadequacy. They just don't see any possibility of their achieving anything in life that will give them any gratification. In desperation, they may turn to the only thing they feel can give them some pleasure in life.

Other youngsters might indeed feel capable of achieving something, but the fruits of their labors are years away. They may see these as not materializing until they have completed graduate school and achieved a modicum of success in a profession or business. But that may be 15 years away! Who can wait that long?

Our technology has provided us with so many instantaneous results that we have lost tolerance for any delay. I still recall when several sheets of carbon paper were the only way to get multiple copies. I stood in wonderment of a machine that could produce 60 clear copies per minute. Now I am told that this machine should be relegated to the junk pile in favor of one that can produce 200 copies a minute. Many people do avail themselves of the costly, more advanced model. Waiting $3^1/_2$ minutes for 200 copies is unthinkable!

With this kind of attitude prevailing, is it any wonder that young people are unwilling to wait 15 years for a lift?

We have two challenges. First, to develop a value system which teaches that there is something else in life other than thrill seeking. We must do everything possible to help our children develop a sense of self-confidence. They must be able to feel capable of achieving these values. Second, they must realize that there are some things worth waiting for. We should learn to tolerate delay.

Eight administrations have fought a losing "war on drugs." I suspect that we will never win this war until we have a sensible and acceptable answer to give young people when they ask, "What else is there?"

For one possible answer, read on.

63

DOING GOOD VS. FEELING GOOD

I was privileged to participate in a tribute dinner honoring a group of volunteers. These were people across the age spectrum, from older adolescents to retirees, who had formed a group to offer an interesting service. They provided a modicum of companionship to "shut-ins."

What are "shut-ins"? These are people who are essentially restricted to their apartments. They are elderly people whose families do not live nearby. Because they suffer from the wear-and-tear conditions of advanced age — poor vision, poor hearing, arthritis — they are confined to their homes. They are unable to drive a car and many have difficulty even walking by themselves. These volunteers donate a few hours each week to spend with them, perhaps take them to the supermarket or to a doctor's office, or for a drive in the countryside, or play cards with them, etc.

On the table were brochures which announced the topic of the evening, "Doing Good vs. Feeling Good." This hit home with me. After all, I was spending my entire workday with people who became addicted to alcohol or drugs primarily because they sought to feel good. The drive to feel good was primary in their lives. What if people were driven primarily to "do good," and "feeling good" became secondary in importance? Is it possible that this might be the solution to the epidemic of chemical dependency?

The more I thought about it, the more convinced I became that I was on the right track. Furthermore, "doing good" results in "feeling good." One may not get a "rush" or a sudden "high" as with drugs, but there is a very good feeling in doing good. And this good feeling may last for months and years instead of the few minutes of euphoria provided by the deadly heroin or cocaine.

The following evening I met with a group of parents of adolescents who were being treated for drug addiction. I was fired up with enthusiasm from the previous evening, and I shared it with them. If we could adopt the goal of "doing good" we might be able to prevent the recourse to drugs.

The following morning one of the staff said, "You really made an impression last night. After you left I heard some parents say, 'The doctor is right. We have to get after our kids to do some volunteering.' "

My heart sank. The parents hadn't heard a thing. You don't get after the kids to do volunteering. You do it yourself! You set an example. On a Sunday morning you might say to your 10-year-old, "I'm going to Mrs. Smith's to take her for a ride or to the supermarket. Want to come along?" The child will know that you could have used that leisure time to relax or to play golf, but that you are giving of yourself to help someone feel better. They (children and grown-ups alike) can learn firsthand that the good feeling that results can persist for a long time. Telling someone how noble it is to volunteer while you lie in the hammock is of no use.

"Doing good" is one answer to the question, "What else is there?" We may not be able to get the entire population of the United States to adopt this attitude, but we might succeed in getting our own family members to accept it. But only if we show them how it's done.

64

DON'T TALK OPERATIONS DURING THE MEAL

Many years ago I accompanied my father to the Mayo Clinic. In the dining room of our hotel there was a prominent sign: **"DON'T TALK OPERATIONS DURING THE MEAL."** Mealtime should be pleasant.

The same holds true in the home. There are all kinds of subjects that can be unpleasant. Things at work can go wrong, there can be problems at school, and there may have been some mishaps involving friends. Make it a point not to bring up anything during mealtime that might lead to something unpleasant.

On some of the supper-time news programs there are commercials for medications to treat indigestion. No wonder! If you watch the news during mealtime you may well end up with indigestion.

In order to avoid potentially unpleasant topics, it is wise to be prepared with something pleasant to talk about. Take some time to prepare a subject for the conversation at mealtime. Perhaps a heartwarming human interest story, or a few jokes, or some biographical material about some sports heroes. Ask the children to take turns in preparing something pleasant to discuss at dinner. But don't make a contest of who has told the funniest joke or the best story. If someone wins, then someone has lost, and that is not pleasant.

But what if you don't have the time to prepare a topic for mealtime talk? Well, then *make* some time for it. It may be more important than many things for which you *do* find time.

Spats are never pleasant. It should be made clear that arguments over anything cannot be brought up during mealtime. Should anyone bring up a controversial issue, suggest postponing it until after the meal. That may mean you can't leave the table immediately after desert. You've got to give the person the opportunity to express whatever you had asked him to postpone.

Mealtime can become a time when everyone gets some emotional nutrition. This can be just as vital to health as the carbohydrates and proteins.

65

SHARING YOUR GOOD FORTUNE

I was really shocked at myself.

I'm not a compulsive gambler, but I do buy a lottery ticket once a week. Why? Because I think that perhaps I am destined to become wealthy, but there is no way that I deserve an outright miracle like digging to plant tomatoes and discovering oil on my property. Therefore I reason that if I provide God with a way to make me wealthy without having to perform a miracle I might succeed.

So far the most I've won is one dollar. One day I was buying my ticket, when the man who was behind me said to the clerk, "I want to be lucky. Give me the same numbers as the rabbi."

I said to the man, "Boy, are you ever mistaken. I haven't had a bit of luck in the last eight years. Try some other numbers."

"No," the man said. "Give me the rabbi's numbers."

I walked away actually harboring a resentment. "Hey, if I do win, I'll have to share the $40 million with this guy! What right does he have to encroach on my winnings?"

My emotions were all mixed up. I thought it was funny that I would not be satisfied with just $20 million. I felt angry at this man who would take half of my winnings. I was disappointed at myself for being so selfish and begrudging someone else.

Maybe that's part of human nature. If so, it is a trait we should dispose of. We should be happy to share our good fortune with others. This is true whether we share a lottery windfall or give a portion of our weekly earnings to charity.

When sharing becomes a pleasure instead of a resented obligation, life becomes more enjoyable.

We want to teach our children how to share. They need to learn this in their early years, when they tend to keep their toys to themselves. Let's show them how we share and enjoy it.

66.

LOOKING FORWARD

The very fact that the term "empty-nest syndrome" exists indicates that it is not an infrequent occurrence. It has its counterpart in a syndrome which, to the best of my knowledge, does not yet have a name. This latter condition happens to retirees. In both cases parents or workers may feel that they don't have much reason to get out of bed in the morning. There are no children to care for and no job to report to.

These conditions result in a rude awakening. Many people eagerly await the day when they will not have to punch the clock. I recall my mother looking forward to the time when she would not have to get up at 2 A.M. to feed her twin babies. She then eagerly awaited elimination of the 6 A.M. feeding. Both the housewife and the worker would like to be free of the stresses and demands on their time and energy. But when the long awaited day arrives, the relief is short lived.

A man whose life was less than exemplary died, and found himself in the most beautiful surroundings imaginable. He was surprised that he had indeed merited a heavenly reward.

Seeing a richly stocked bar, he wished to pour himself a drink. A uniformed servant appeared at his side. "What is your wish?" he asked. The man told him his favorite drink, which was promptly served. He was about to reach for a book when again a servant appeared and handed him the desired volume. When he wanted to help himself from the sumptuous table decked with delicacies, he was again served. Every time he wished to do anything, a servant appeared and did it for him. After a while the man asked the servants to go away. "Let me do something myself," he said.

"I'm sorry, sir." the servant said. "The only thing that is forbidden here is for you to do anything. You just tell us what you would like and we will do it for you."

"This is absurd," the man said. "If I can't do anything myself, I'd rather be in Hell."

"And just where do you think you are?" the servant said.

We may think that being free of all responsibility is bliss. Retirees and parents whose children have all left home have found otherwise.

This needn't be the case. There is much one can do when free of one's usual work. The empty-nest syndrome can be prevented. We begin to plan for financial security 40 years in advance. We should also begin to plan for our leisure years well in advance.

The world is a fascinating place. There is so much to know and learn. Torah scholars find that the words of *Psalms* are true:

"They shall blossom in their old age" (32:15). There is history, literature, and the arts. There are faraway places and wonders of nature. These can be visited on video if one cannot physically get there. We get but a tiny fragment of world knowledge in our formal education. The leisure years is when we can catch up.

There is no dearth of people who can benefit from one's help. One can easily find places where one can volunteer.

The most common mistake people make is to so lose themselves in their daily activities that they give no thought to the future. They naively assume that leisure is enjoyable. It can be very enjoyable, but only if we think ahead and prepare ourselves for those wonderful days when our time will be our own.

67

SHE THINKS I'M REAL!

hildren want to know that they are important.

Parents took their 6-year-old child to the restaurant. The waitress took the parents' orders. She then turned to the child. "What will you have?"

"Two hot dogs with lots of mustard and a coke," the child said.

Mother smiled to the waitress. "You can bring him roast beef with mashed potatoes and vegetables," she said.

The waitress returned and served the parents what they had ordered. Before the child she placed two hot dogs with mustard and a coke. The mother was shocked, but the little boy grinned from ear to ear. "Look, Mommy," he said. "She thinks I'm real!"

If children are not given an opportunity to express their individuality, they may see themselves as being only appendages to their parents, but not having an existence of their own.

A child should be allowed to make choices. "What would you like to wear today?" If he chooses unwisely, you can say, "That's too heavy for today's weather," or "Let's save that for when we

155

go out." If you have no reason to disagree with his choice, why are you disapproving of it?

Similarly, children can occasionally be asked what they would like for supper. You can explain why supper cannot consist of ice cream and popcorn. Among healthy foods, why should they not have some say in what they eat? If their choice requires too much preparation, you can say, "I'd love to make that for you, but I don't have enough time today. We'll have that on another day, O.K.?"

Obviously there are decisions which children are incapable of making. However, if you show them that you respect their opinions in things which they can decide, they are much more likely to defer to your wisdom in areas beyond their scope.

68.

LET IT HURT

It is not unusual to find that in their old age some people become cantankerous. Nothing seems to satisfy them. We may be irritated by their apparent lack of appreciation for what we are trying to do for them.

When I was an intern, I was often called to administer intravenous medications. (In those days there were no IV nurses.) I responded to one call to find that the patient was Mrs. Glass.

I had known Mrs. Glass all my life. She had been president of the Ladies Auxiliary of my father's congregation even before I was born. She had undergone amputation of both legs because of gangrene. She was 88 and resided in the home for the aged. She had been hospitalized for pneumonia.

Mrs. Glass recognized me and was happy to see me. I told her I was going to give her an injection. "It won't hurt much," I said. "Just a tiny prick of a needle."

Mrs. Glass responded, "Foolish child! Let it hurt! Do you think one wants to leave a world that is pleasant?"

I have often thought about her wise words. The best thing that can happen on a vacation is for the last two days to be dreary, wet, and cold. Going back home is actually a relief. If the last two days are bright and sunny, and you can go swimming or play golf, going back to the drudgery of the office can be very unpleasant.

What Mrs. Glass was saying is that as she was approaching the end of her life, it was easier to accept leaving the world if she could see it as a miserable place to be.

I came to understand that the cantankerousness of the elderly can be defensive. They really do appreciate what we do for them. They just can't afford to feel satisfied.

Many visiting nurses have told me that their patients may berate them and criticize everything they do. Yet, when they leave, the patient asks, "Will you be coming back soon?"

If we understand why some people complain, we may be able to tolerate it much better.

69.

USE AND DISCARD

Sometimes I wonder. In history we learn about the Stone Age, the Bronze Age, etc. What will our era be called? "The Throwaway Age." Just look at how many things we have that are disposable. Paper plates, cups, forks and spoons, tissues, napkins, tablecloths, diapers, syringes, etc. We now have disposable cameras and contact lenses!

Things were not always this way. For my Bar Mitzvah I received a Sheaffer fountain pen that served me faithfully for 20 years. When it was lost, I felt I had lost something that had meaning to me, even if it was only an inanimate object. Today I have a drawer full of ballpoint pens, most of which were promotional giveaways. I couldn't care less if one or more were lost.

I remember taking a radio to be repaired. If you tried to do this today you would be considered to be crazy. You don't repair a broken radio! You throw it away and get a new one. Even the automobile for which you paid thousands of dollars is not likely to remain yours for long. If you can afford it, you'll trade it in after three years. Why? Because.

What am I getting at? Our culture has developed an attitude that rather than try and fix something, it is more convenient to throw it away and get a new one. So what? *This attitude may actually carry over to relationships.* Are there problems with the marriage? Well, discard the spouse and get a new one!

The incidence of broken homes is unprecedented. How can it be that two people who were once so attracted to each other that they were ready to make a lifelong commitment have become so incompatible? Granted, something may have gone wrong with the relationship. But with some time and effort things might be repaired. Sure. But why spend time and effort on fixing something when you can get a new one?

"Absurd!" you may say. Well, the impact of subliminal stimuli has been proven. This is no different. There has been a subtle indoctrination to an attitude of "Don't bother fixing something when you can get a new one."

I'm not saying that we must go back to cloth napkins and expensive fountain pens. However, we should be aware that we may have inadvertently fallen prey to a wrong attitude. People are not objects. If something goes awry in a relationship, whether between friends or between husband and wife, we should do everything possible to see if it can be fixed.

Medical science has indeed given us the magic of organ transplants. It is only when a heart or kidney is irreparably diseased that we may replace it. How foolish it would be if one sought a kidney transplant because of a mild kidney infection!

A repaired clothes dryer may not be as good as a new one. But a restored relationship that was initiated with love is much better than a new one.

70.

KIDS NEED PRIVACY TOO

We may not think of it, but kids need privacy too. We don't like the children to rummage through our things. Why not accord them the same respect?

Obviously there may be space limitations which restrict the area that can be private. But even in the most crowded dwelling a child can have a little chest with a lock to which he alone holds the key. It gives a child a much needed feeling of esteem, knowing that his territory is acknowledged and respected.

No. Privacy is not the same as keeping secrets. "Daddy and Mommy have valuable and important papers which we keep in a safe place. You can have a place where you can keep things that are valuable and important to you."

Sometimes it may be necessary to exercise parental authority and investigate the area of privacy. A child may deny having sequestered a sibling's yo-yo. If the parent suspects that it is in the locked compartment, it may be necessary to have a look. You might explain to the child that if the police suspect a person may be concealing something, they may get a search warrant. You might even write out a little "search warrant" and hand it to the child. You may explain that when something is missing, one must look everywhere. If the yo-yo should be found in the child's possession, it can be pointed out that privacy is a privilege. If a privilege is abused it will be taken away. Taking the yo-yo and lying about it was very wrong. The child can have his private area but must realize that it is given to him because he is trustworthy, and it is expected that he will not misuse this privilege.

Without any privacy at all, a child may not have a proper sense of individuality. He is just another object in the house.

If you do give the child some privacy and respect it, you may be well rewarded with the increased respect he has for *your* privacy.

71.

GROW TOGETHER OR RISK GROWING APART

The following insight came about as a result of my work with alcoholics, but I believe that much the same can occur in any marriage, even where there is no alcohol problem. In fact, it can occur where there is no problem at all.

When an alcoholic recovers, it is not enough that he stops drinking. Unless he undergoes some very major character changes, he is likely to drink again. He must do a moral inventory and rid himself of his character defects. He must make amends to those whom he has harmed or offended. He must be ready to admit mistakes promptly rather than defend them. He must try to help others who wish to recover, and he must become more spiritual. He accomplishes these changes by participating in the meetings of the 12-step program and with the guidance of someone with experience in recovery.

There is an analogous program for family members and particularly the spouse of the alcoholic. They have invariably suffered from the person's alcoholism, and should know how to adjust to the changes. Quite often the spouse may say, "My husband needs this program to keep him from drinking. I don't have a problem. There's no need for me to go to any meetings."

What may happen is that over a period of years the husband grows in character and spirituality, while the wife remains stagnant. This may result in a disparity which may threaten their compatibility. While the wife may not have needed the program for a "problem," she could have benefited from the personal growth it provides.

It should be obvious that a similar disparity can occur in any relationship where only one partner progresses. The progress may consist of spiritual growth, of changing goals in life, of changing interests, of looking for different associations with friends, of becoming more assertive, etc. If the other partner does not progress correspondingly, he/she may have a different goal, may not share interests, may not wish to develop different friendships, and may have wanted a more passive rather than an assertive spouse. The two may find themselves growing apart. Sometimes the relationship becomes a "peaceful coexistence." If the gap is too wide, even that becomes untenable.

This does not mean that a husband and wife must be identical in every way. To the contrary, the excitement in the relationship may be due to the ways in which they differ. However, if a relationship was formed on the basis of certain terms, in this case the character traits of each partner, and the latter undergo more than minor changes, the basis of the relationship may disintegrate.

It would be a shame if marriages continued only because both partners did not grow. If only one grows, there can be problems. It is therefore desirable that both partners grow, and take an interest in each other's growth.

72.

ADD FLAVOR TO YOUR LIFE

I t is easy to understand why a person may wish to protect himself from painful feelings. But why would anyone want to avoid good feelings? I found the answer, but it cost me $111!

The laundry tub in my basement kept dripping, and this is one of the things than is generally O.K. to "do yourself" (remember?). In order to replace the washer, I had to turn off the water pipe to the spigot. Try as I might, I couldn't turn off the valve. I could have used a wrench, but that is one of the things to *not* do yourself. Too great a danger of breaking the pipe. So I did the only sensible thing. I called a plumber.

I felt vindicated when the plumber could not turn the valve either. "That valve has probably not been turned since this house was built 75 years ago," he said. "It's stuck. Frozen. If I try to force it I might break the pipe. (See? I was right!) The only thing to do is to turn off the main valve. but that will shut off the water supply to everything in the house." I didn't have much choice. So we'd be without water for a half hour.

The plumber shut off the main valve. A few minutes later he appeared holding the spigot. "Bad news, Doc. It's not the washer. The whole inside of the faucet is worn out. Need a new faucet. I haven't got one like this on the truck. Need to go back to the shop."

By the time the new faucet was replaced and the main valve turned back on, over three hours had elapsed. The repair cost me $111. When I turned on a faucet anywhere in the house, I was jolted by an explosive discharge of dirty water.

Two days later I was consulted by a man who complained of not having any feelings. He could not experience joy, pride, or love. I learned that when he was ten, his father died suddenly of a heart attack. He remembered looking in the mirror and saying to himself, "You are *not* going to cry." And he didn't.

It became evident that he had tried to defend himself against the pain of grief. He wanted to turn off the "valve" that controls grief. However, he couldn't find that valve. The only thing he could do was, like the plumber, shut off the main valve that controls *all* emotions. For many years he had been devoid of feelings.

In order to feel anything, including pleasant feelings, he would have to open that main valve and allow himself to feel. However, like the explosive discharges of water, he felt threatened that opening the valve might result in a sudden surge of feelings that might overwhelm him. There are cases where people have died from sudden good news. He felt that he had to defend himself against *all* emotions.

Feelings are the flavor of life. If you are unable to experience feelings, get some expert help. You may have had a valid reason for turning off the main valve. However, you should not let yourself be deprived of the many good feelings that life has to offer.

73.

GREAT EXPECTATIONS

aving your first baby is full of thrills: the joy of seeing a little human being that you produced; the grandparents swearing that this is the most beautiful child ever born, and the smartest, too, at four days! Thrills come by the bundle.

Of course, there are a few minor bumps. You are no longer free to leave the house whenever you wish. You just can't pick up and go away for the weekend like you used to. But these are insignificant. Furthermore, you knew full well that the baby would bring these restrictions, and you gladly accepted them.

However, what you might not have considered (why should you have?) is that your baby might be colicky. After being fed, burped, and diapered, the baby is in misery. Even pacing the floor with him doesn't help. The child's writhing indicates he is in pain. You take the baby to the pediatrician, who does not appear to be the least bit concerned. Why should he be? He doesn't have to watch the child cry.

"He's alright, mother. That's the way some babies are. He'll get over it. Don't worry." When you pressure the doctor to do something, he may suggest a change in formula. You do it, but it doesn't help.

Believe the doctor. He's right. The child *will* outgrow it, with no residual scars. That is, if you let him.

But suppose you just can't sit by and do nothing. Especially if you believe that the baby's crying means that you are doing something wrong. You think you're not a good mother. That's what your husband must be thinking, right? And what is your mother-in-law going to think of you as a mother?

In desperation you call your friend. She has had three children. She must know what to do. "The baby must be constipated," Ethel says. "Give him a glycerin suppository." Sounds like a good idea. Trouble is, it doesn't work. You didn't want your mother to find out about this, but you have no other choice. Tearfully you call her. "Mom, there's something wrong with the baby. He won't stop crying."

"He's teething, honey," Mom says. (At five weeks?) Rub some paregoric on his gums." That may just work. Paregoric is opium. If you put enough of it on his gums, it'll stop his crying. In fact, if *you* took enough of the paregoric, you wouldn't care about the baby's crying.

You've already done too many things to the baby. If you keep on asking for more advice from different people, that little baby will have more done to him in a day than he should experience all year!

If your pediatrician tells you the baby's fine and that nothing needs to be done, trust him. Colic is one of the "bumps" in being a new parent. You can smooth out this bump by following your doctor's advice. If there is nothing to do, he'll outgrow it.

74.

YOU ARE LOVABLE

One of the consequences of low self-esteem is that a person may have doubts that he can really be loved. This is a feeling that can haunt a person. It may affect his thinking and behavior, even though he may not be conscious that he feels this way about himself. A husband may feel insecure, living in fear that he may be rejected or abandoned. He may feel that he does not deserve to be loved. Obviously, although we have been referring to "he," this may be equally true of the wife.

It is wonderful for a husband to be thoughtful and helpful, and to give his wife gifts, even when it is not a special occasion. He should do these things out of love and consideration for her, and to give her pleasure. These should *not* be done because of fear of her abandoning him. He should not feel that he must compensate because he is inadequate. The acts are right, but the motivation is wrong.

Ruth consulted me because her husband had undergone a marked personality change so severe that their marriage was in jeopardy.

Milton and Ruth had an apparently happy marriage of 16 years. Milton was a successful home builder. Ruth was a very bright and efficient woman. When the youngest of their four children began attending school all day, she took a course in real estate and earned a realtor's license. Milton was very supportive, and felt that this would complement his home-building business.

After Ruth made several successful sales and received her commission, Milton's attitude changed remarkably. He became very critical. When she went to show a home to a prospective buyer, he objected. "You have no business going out at night. It's dangerous!" If she had clients on a Sunday, he would say, "You belong home with the children on the weekend." He tried to "help" Ruth on several home sales, but effectively sabotaged the deals. Whereas he had always had a pleasant demeanor, he became grouchy and short-tempered. Ruth was afraid that he might have a brain tumor that was causing this personality change. Medical examination showed otherwise.

Milton came for an evaluation. I found him to have a serious self-esteem problem — he did not feel that he was lovable. He was very insecure about Ruth's love for him. Why would such a wonderful woman like Ruth want someone like him for a husband? He had concluded that the only reason she had remained with him was because he provided economic security for her and the children. But if Ruth were successful in real estate and became financially independent, she would have little use for him. Her assertions that she loved him did not reassure him.

Milton saw Ruth's business as a threat. This is why he objected to it and tried to undermine it.

With therapy directed at overcoming his poor self-concept, Milton's insecurity faded. He was able to accept Ruth's love as genuine, and the happiness of their marriage was not only restored, but greatly enhanced.

Feelings of "unlovableness" are not at all uncommon. They may be masked by a variety of psychological defenses. Overcoming the faulty self-perception that causes such feelings will lead to greater happiness.

At a retreat, I discussed the "unlovableness" problem. One couple had their baby with them. The grandparents were there too, and the baby was cuddled and kissed by everyone. Having heard my lecture, the mother said to the baby, "And don't you dare tell a psychologist 20 years from now that you feel unlovable because you were deprived of love as a child!"

There are no guarantees, but if children are shown much love, they are less likely to feel unlovable as adults.

75.

SPOIL 'EM ROTTEN AND GIVE 'EM BACK

It's wonderful to be a grandparent. You can enjoy the grandchildren, spoil them, and then give them back to their parents.

My father was crazy about his grandchildren. When I would bring my children over, his face would light up. He played with them, kissed them, gave them candy, and let them romp around a bit. Then he would take them by the hand, bring them to me and say, "Are these yours?" I knew that meant I was to take them home. My father would say, "When G-d made it so that you don't have small children after 50, He knew what He was doing."

I never had any doubt about how much my father loved my children. I realized, however, that as you approach becoming a senior citizen, you may lose the requisite patience to put up with juvenile behavior. When I became a grandfather, that became very clear to me.

There are times when grandparents should lend a hand for

175

longer periods of time, as when the parents go on vacation and they are asked to look after the grandchildren. That is doable. There may be other situations when grandparents must make a greater investment. As a rule, however, grandparents should provide much love, kisses, candy, and take kids to the zoo or on other outings. They may also help the grandchildren realize that their parents were also little at one time.

Esther may tell Grandma on coming home from school, "Mommy's going to kill me! I got a 60 in arithmetic."

Grandma may say, "Honey, if you pay more attention to your schoolwork, your grades will be much better. But don't worry about Mommy killing you. I didn't kill her when she got a 60 on her test. I just made her do her homework better."

Esther will smile from ear to ear. She will be much better prepared for her mother's rebuke. And she is more likely to improve her grades than if the rebuke had not been mitigated.

Let's face it. Grandparents may sometimes cause "bumps." But they smooth out many more than they cause.

Maybe that's how the term "grand-parents" came to be. They are parents who are grand.

76

THE JUVENILE COLLUSION

I don't think that children actually put their heads together and conspire. But if they did, it could not result in a more efficient collusion.

"But Mike's mother lets him (do whatever it is you just refused)." The implication is that you are being unduly harsh and restrictive. You don't want to be thought of as a shrew, so you give in. I wager that perhaps at this very moment Mike is requesting what you have just refused on the basis that "you let." Mothers rarely call one another to verify the claim that other mothers "let."

When the children reach their teens, this takes on a much more serious proportion. The thought of your child being friendless and shunned by his peers may overwhelm your better judgment.

Don't get taken in by this tactic. Tell your children that you have given their request serious consideration (which you should do), and you have come to a decision. Your decision will not be affected by what others do. The only thing that can change your decision is being shown that it is incorrect on its own merits. With all due respect to other parents, you must decide for yourself what is right and wrong.

Parents of the neighborhood, unite! Get together and decide ground rules, and then stick by them. It may be tough when your children fault you for being so inconsiderate and making them into social outcasts. You can make it much less tough on yourself by getting together and establishing a united front. Whatever the request is, if you have good reason to deny it, stand firm. Your decision will benefit the children.

77

NO ONE TO CARE FOR

Of course family members should care for one another. That's what families are for. However, caring should be role appropriate. When it's not, things may not seem tough at the beginning, but may end up tougher than you think.

Ethel was the oldest in the family. For whatever reason, Ethel's mother abdicated the care of the younger children. Ethel was essentially the mother to her three younger siblings when she was nine. She continued to serve as their mother until they married. Ethel's father was a meek man. He saw no reason to change things when everything was running so smoothly.

Ethel married and had two children. She cared for them, while still being available to her siblings. Ethel cared for everyone, except for herself. She never had time to develop any outside interests. Her life consisted of caring for others. This gave her a real sense of worth.

When her children married, Ethel cared for her husband. When he developed heart disease, Ethel cared for him. She was in her 60s when her husband died.

I was the fourth psychiatrist whom Ethel consulted for treatment of her severe depression. All available treatments had not brought about any improvement. The reason for Ethel's depression was quite evident. She felt there was no point to living. She had no one to care for.

Just one block from Ethel's home there was an active senior citizen's center. Ethel reluctantly went there a few times. None of the activities interested her. Ethel had never become accustomed to any kind of frivolous pastimes. There was only one thing that gave her any feeling of well-being: taking care of someone. Volunteering at a hospital was not the same.

Some people might consider caring for others as a tough burden. It was not at all tough for Ethel. It was the only thing she knew how to do.

We should teach our children to care for others. But even the noble trait of caring must be in proper proportion.

Neither selfishness nor self-negation are virtuous. The great sage Hillel summed it up thusly: "If I am not for myself, then who will be for me? But if I am only for myself, of what good am I?" If we are both for ourselves and for others, life need not be tough.

78.

LOOK FOR THE SILVER LINING

Perhaps not all clouds have silver linings, but many of them do. If you look closely, you will find that things you had considered to be terrible when they occurred later proved to be to your advantage. One may lose a housekeeper of many years, a secretary, or any other employee, and feel that the bottom has dropped out. How can I ever replace her? Then one finds that the replacement is four times as efficient! How often has it happened that someone who thought that his world had come to an end when he lost his job got a much better one? Sure, we would rather have blessings that are not in disguise. However, if we will only bear in mind that some previous "calamities" were indeed blessings in disguise, some hardships can be borne with less suffering.

One recovering alcoholic said, "I began to see a pattern in my life. When bad things happened, they were most often a prelude to something good. Now when something bad happens, I am excited and eager to see what good is going to occur."

The comic strip character "Ziggy" is always the victim of bad things happening to him. Yet even Ziggy can find some consolation in some of the bad things.

What can be worse than pain?

Pain may be the only way in which some people can be brought to their senses. Many people feel that they are the "boss" of their own lives and that they are in control of everything. They may refuse to recognize their vulnerability as mortals. Consequently, they may never give serious consideration to their behavior or to what they should be accomplishing in their lifetime. It may take some pain to bring them to their senses so that they can live a more responsible life.

Of course, there are some happenings in which we cannot possibly see any silver lining. Overcoming these requires profound faith. Moral support from family and friends can help a person survive difficult ordeals. However, there are things which do have a redeeming feature. We might do well to make a list of things that turned out to be beneficial even though they initially seemed terrible. If we can keep these in mind, some things do not have to be as tough as they seem.

It is important to study the great works that teach decent and ethical behavior. It is even more effective to observe people who behave decently and ethically and emulate them.

79

EVERYONE NEEDS TO FEEL IMPORTANT

Jack and Ann were definitely *not* in a marriage that was made in heaven.

I knew more about Jack because he was my patient. His mother died when he was a child. His stepmother did not take kindly to him, and he received little love from his father. He was determined to succeed in life. He worked his way through college and developed a profitable small business.

I did not know much about Ann's background other than that she came from a wealthy family. She had apparently not been popular. She used to withdraw from people. From Jack's description, she had very poor self-esteem and was insecure.

Jack and Ann both suffered from feelings of inferiority. Jack would try to escape from these distressing feelings by boasting about his achievements in business. Ann's method of feeling better about herself was to belittle other people's accomplishments. If she degraded others, she could see herself as being superior to them.

So here is a typical scenario. Jack comes home all excited about a profitable business transaction he had made that day. Ann says, "Hmph! Big deal. My brother makes much larger transactions than that several times a day. He never even mentions them."

Or: Jack is elated. "Do you know with whom I had lunch today? Earl Gillespie (a sports broadcaster)!" To which Ann responds, "So what? So he talks on the radio. What's so good about that?"

When Ann would put Jack down, his self-esteem was further depressed, and he would react by more boasting. This would prompt another negative comment by Ann. This resulted in a vicious cycle, with misery being heaped atop of misery.

Everyone needs to feel important. We should be alert when people appear to be doing things to impress us. They are probably starved for recognition. If we can help them feel better about themselves, they may be able to dispense with some self-defeating behaviors. This is especially important with children. I recommend the book *Building Self-Esteem in Children,* by Dr. Berne, for anyone who relates to children: parents, grandparents, and teachers. Improvement of self-esteem is of great benefit to the entire family.

80.

DAYDREAMS

We sometimes daydream about the future. Dreaming can be constructive, as long as we return to the world of reality and don't get lost in fantasyland. We may dream about goals we wish to reach, and these dreams may motivate us to do the things that will make them reality.

Visualizing the future can help alleviate some kinds of stress. Say your 8-month-old child is teething, and awakens you at 3 A.M. You walk him, and when you think he has fallen asleep and you put him into his crib, he immediately starts crying again. He finally falls asleep at 5 A.M. You have to be up at 6 A.M. to make it to the office on time.

These early morning hours walking the baby can be stressful. It might help if you allow yourself to visualize the future. One day this little boy or girl will give you great pride when he/she graduates. You will be radiating joy as you escort him/her to the wedding ceremony. These difficult wee morning hours will fade into meaninglessness in light of the joy this child will bring.

On the other hand, there is the story of the mother who was worried about her son leaving home to go to school. How will he react if he does not make good grades? Will he give up and lose interest in higher education? What kind of friends will he have? What happens if those friends use drugs?

As she was pondering this, she heard him crying. So she changed his diaper.

There is no point in worrying unnecessarily about the future. Such worrying will not contribute to any positive outcome. Why project misery when you can anticipate joy?

Needless worry can become a self-fulfilling prophecy. An attitude of anxiety and depression may wear off onto the child and hinder his progress.

Should you think about the future? Yes. *Happily!*

81.

THE ENDLESS WAIT

There are few things in life that can be as aggravating as waiting for the plumber or electrician who promised to be at your home in the morning and never showed up at all that day. We call very angrily and say, "Do you realize that I rearranged my whole week so that I could be at home? I can't take off another day!" I'm not sure what you mean by that last statement. Of course you're going to take off another day. You want the plumbing and electricity to be repaired, don't you?

I can understand how this may happen. I had an electrician come for what appeared to be a minor problem. It turned out to be much more complicated than he thought. He could not drop everything and run to the next job. The people who were expecting him had to be disappointed and even angry.

Let me suggest this: When your repairman tells you when he expects to be at your home, say, "I understand that unforseen things may happen that may delay you. If you see that happening, please call me so that I won't be sitting on pins and needles."

This usually works. If you show him some understanding, he is much more likely to remember to call you. You may be able to salvage the rest of the day.

It is true, you pay him for his work. Don't forget to offer him a cold drink in summer or coffee in winter. If you are satisfied with his work, tell him that you will recommend him to your friends, as you indeed should.

Waiting endlessly for a repairman to show up may be tough. It does not have to be all that tough. In all likelihood, you may have need for his services again. Relate to him decently the first time. You will be less frustrated on future occasions.

82.

PUT YOUR MASK ON FIRST

Hey, Mom and Dad! Do you feel guilty when you go out for an evening and the kids are crying that they don't want to be with a babysitter? Or if you drop the kids off at your mother's place or with friends and go away for a few days? Can you enjoy yourself, or are you reprimanding yourself for having "abandoned" your children?

Well, you should learn to get rid of the guilt and enjoy yourself. First of all, you need it. Second, you'll do more for the children if you get away for awhile.

Have you traveled by airplane? The flight attendant instructs you how to put on the oxygen masks if there is a loss of cabin pressure. Then she says, "If you are traveling with a child, put your own mask on first and then assist the child."

What kind of mother would be so selfish as to take care of herself first? Wouldn't a responsible mother give the child the oxygen first?

If she does that while not having enough oxygen for herself, she may become so confused that she will improperly place the mask on the child. Both of them will then be deprived of oxygen. In order to provide oxygen for the child, she must put on her own mask first.

That should serve as a prototype for parents. If they do not keep themselves in optimal condition, both physically and emotionally, they cannot provide well for their children

You may need time for yourselves. You may need a few days away from the kids so that you can hear yourself think. Regardless of how much the children may protest, you will be doing them a favor by allowing yourself to relax.

83

DIFFERENT STROKES FOR DIFFERENT FOLKS

The Talmud relates that the great sage Hillel told his students that going to the bathhouse was a *mitzvah*. "What kind of a *mitzvah* is that?" they asked. "Do they not wash the statue, the likeness of the emperor, to honor him?" Hillel responded. "Since man was created in the likeness of G-d, we must honor G-d by respecting His image. When I go to the bathhouse, I am cleansing the Divine image. Also, my real self is my soul, and it is housed within the body. I must therefore show my body appreciation for its hospitality toward my soul."

How different our lives would be if, like Hillel, we conceptualized ourselves as being in the Divine image, and of being grateful to our bodies for containing our souls!

How ironic it is to see a person smoking a cigarette while washing or waxing his car. He exerts himself to protect and beautify his car while he inflicts damage on his body by smoking. Does the body not merit at least as much care as one's automobile?

Hillel teaches us that keeping the body healthy and attractive is a *mitzvah*. It is a way in which we express our reverence of G-d. Anything we do that may harm our body is nothing less than an affront against G-d.

When we eat healthy foods we are doing a *mitzvah*. When we exercise to improve our circulation and to strengthen our muscles we are doing a *mitzvah*. When we avoid the indulgences that can injure the body we are doing a *mitzvah*.

If we act in a way that shows we consider the body to be a sacred shrine, we not only fulfill the *mitzvah* of honoring G-d, but we also set an example for our children. This may be a very effective method of preventing our children from falling prey to the epidemic of drug use that prevails among young people. Let's teach our children to protect the Divine image, or, in other words, themselves.

84

REALITY CHECK

A distraught mother was in anguish because her 16-year-old daughter had left home and had fallen into drug use and undesirable behavior. She was helpless to do anything about it. She had no legal recourse. She had three other children, but was unable to tend adequately to them because of her preoccupation with the errant daughter.

When she met with other parents of wayward children, they told her that she must accept the fact that her daughter was beyond her control. The mother said to me, "I'll never accept that!"

"You mean you think you can do something about it?" I asked.

"No, I know I can't. But I still cannot accept it."

"Let's clarify terms," I said. "What you mean is that you do not and will not *approve* of what she is doing. You also do not wish to give up hope that she will one day come to her senses and abandon her self-destructive behavior. You are right on both accounts. However, 'acceptance' does not mean 'approval' nor does it mean 'despair.' Acceptance means acknowledging facts for what they are. As of today, you must accept the unfortunate fact that you cannot do anything to rescue your daughter, and you certainly do not approve of it. Perhaps things may change tomorrow.

"If you accept this fact today, you will be able to devote your energies to your other children who need a mother's care. If you deny reality and insist on doing something at a time when nothing can be done, you will deplete yourself in futile actions."

There are many things in life of which we disapprove, but they are facts nevertheless. If we do not confuse acceptance with approval, we may be able to continue to function in the face of adversity.

85

MAKING CREASES

If you are a veteran in marriage, skip this article. It is intended for newlyweds or prospective husbands and wives.

Do this simple exercise. Take a piece of rigid corrugated cardboard and fold one corner. Now straighten it out. Smooth out the fold as much as you wish, even using a flat-iron. You will notice that at the place where there was a fold, there is a crease. Nothing you can do can make that crease disappear.

Now put some pressure on any part of the cardboard. You will find that there is resistance, and it does not bend easily. Now apply just a little pressure to the place where there had once been a fold. You will notice that it bends rather easily.

What's the point of this? Any experience or feeling that is impressive, traumatic, or otherwise, results in sensitivity that allows for easy arousal of that feeling. Even a slight stimulus may bring back that initial feeling. This is the "recall" phenomenon.

If you have ever gone back to the place where you had an accident or a narrow escape, you know what the recall phenomenon is. You again experience the terrifying sensation you felt during the initial accident.

Early in marriage, husbands and wives may not be aware of each other's sensitivities. They may say something which they think is a joke, but which touches a raw nerve. Or they may have a spat, or say something critical of the other. This may result in a painful sensation, which now becomes a "crease." Weeks, months, and even years later, a totally innocent remark may serve as a trigger to bring back that original unpleasant sensation.

It is therefore important, particularly in the early phases of a relationship, to make every effort to avoid making "creases." In addition, we should try to understand what "creases" may have occurred prior to the marriage that may have rendered a person excruciatingly sensitive. This can eliminate much unnecessary distress.

Finally, if you have had an experience which left you with a "crease," be aware of your increased sensitivity. If someone touches you after you have sustained a severe sunburn, you do not impart a hostile motive to that person even though he caused you to have pain. Rather, you realize that the pain was due to the sensitivity of your skin. That's what you should think when you feel offended by something your spouse said or did. As with the touch to the sunburn, do not react with anger to what may be an innocent remark.

86

EGO TRIPS

Cars are the reason for many parent-adolescent disputes. The young man (or woman) may want a car of his own, or wish to borrow the family car. The parents may refuse the request. They may tell him about other ways to get around, such as a bike or bus, or offer to drive him. This may be met with much resistance and anger.

There may be valid reasons for the parental refusal. However, the question is whether they understand what the youngster is asking for. He is *not* asking for a means of transportation. He is asking for something that is very important to his ego. Sitting behind the wheel of a car gives a young person a feeling of power. Being seen driving a car gives him a feeling of being a "somebody." He has a need to impress others.

You may refuse the request, but don't tell him about bikes or being driven. Let him know you understand how important this is for him, but that you just can't afford the substantial increase in insurance premiums. Children can realize that there are things some family members would like to have but cannot afford.

Cars can provide ego inputs for young people. For that matter, they do so for adults as well. People who drive very expensive luxury automobiles could get to their destination just as well with a car that costs less than half as much. If grownups need cars for their ego, why should they expect young people to be different?

You may not succeed in placating your son or daughter with the explanation that you cannot afford the insurance or by offering other reasons why you don't want them driving. But at least you will be talking the same language and *to* each other rather than past each other. This may not eliminate the bumps, but it can smooth them out a bit.

87

A MESSY HOME IS NOT TRAGIC

It can be very aggravating to have things strewn all around the house. The kids just can't seem to get it through their heads that their toys belong in the toy box and the clothes in the closet. If we have told them once not to play ball in the house, we've told them a hundred times. In one ear and out the other. Catching the ball took precedence over caution not to break the vase.

Very aggravating indeed. I attended a meeting at the home of a doctor friend. The house was impeccably clean. Expensive Steuben glass figurines and delicate porcelain statuettes gave the room a very elegant look. These very fragile items were in no danger of being broken. Why? There were no children. A messy house is aggravating. This house was tragic.

I'm not advocating letting the children run wild. Children require discipline and need to learn responsibility, and we must look for ways in which they can be taught to do their fair share. You have every right to be upset by their failure to heed your instructions. Upset, yes. Sad, no. Sad is when you can have precious fragile things all over the house.

88.

FAMILY, NOT FAMILY INC.

My father was a very wise man. He served as counselor to countless people with all sorts of problems. He used to say, "Family members should share festive occasions, not businesses."

Sure, there are any number of businesses that are operated by members of the same family. However, the grief that may possibly result from interfamily conflict when several family members are in the same business should be taken into consideration before embarking on such an arrangement.

Let me cite two scenarios. Two brothers inherited their father's business. One was very diligent, generating more business and investing much time in his work. The other brother took things much easier, relaxing whenever possible. They both drew the same salary. The wife of the more diligent brother felt this was grossly unfair. Why was the other brother entitled to more than his efforts were worth? This caused some strained feelings to develop.

The first brother's wife prevailed upon her husband to tell his brother that unless he shared the load equally he would have to take a cut in his salary. This infuriated the latter's wife, who felt that her husband was doing his fair share. Eventually the family was torn asunder, and the more diligent brother paid the other to leave. By this time the two families were not on speaking terms. Had the business been divided initially, the two families could have remained close.

Another scenario occurred when one family member brought his son into the business. Another family member wanted to bring *his* son in. The latter was not at all business minded and really was not interested in the business. His father insisted on his joining, which turned out to be most unwise. Emotions grew hot, and again much animosity developed within the family.

Rational thought does not always prevail when there are intense emotions. Family members may feel that they are not receiving their due share. When one family member is driving a more expensive automobile than the other, evidence justifying this inequality may have no impact whatsoever. Accusations and counter-accusations may develop.

When family members pursue their fortunes independently of others, they can remain close and share family events together. Everyone ends up much happier.

89

WHO'S IN CONTROL HERE?

Watch a mother feeding her 8-month-old infant. When the mother tries to give him a spoonful of cereal, he clamps his mouth shut. Mother then tries to distract him in ingenious ways, and when he opens his mouth, she quickly shoves in the spoon. The child then holds the food in his mouth, refusing to swallow it. Again the mother distracts him, and when the food hits the pharynx, there is an automatic swallowing reflex. The procedure is repeated with the next spoonful.

Perhaps the child is not hungry, you may say. If the mother answers the phone and forgets to remove the dish, she will find on her return that the baby dug into the food with both hands, trying to get it into his mouth. Why then did he refuse it when his mother fed him? *Because he did not want her to control his eating. He wants to be independent, at eight months!*

Inasmuch as he must eat, he loses this struggle. But when it comes to being toilet-trained, he is defiant. He will show her that she cannot make him do anything that he does not want to do. He resists being controlled.

Eventually this bright child realizes that he is too small to get things on his own and is dependent on his parents to give him the things he wants. However, the parents have their price. They want him to obey them. The child negotiates an unspoken contract. "I'll do what you want. You give me what I want." The parents mistake the child's obedience as their having control of him. Nothing doing! As soon as he is big enough to get things on his own, the terms of the contract are over. He does what he wants.

"What has happened to our child who was always so obedient?" the parents wonder. Nothing has happened to him. It is just that the terms on which the contract was based have changed.

Parental "control" of a child is illusory. The sooner parents recognize this, the better prepared they will be when the child asserts his independence. If they hang onto the belief that they control the child, they may be in for a rude awakening and much turmoil. Dealing with maturing children may be tough, but it will not be as tough if parents do not delude themselves into believing that they are in control.

90

COURT SETTLEMENT

"That's mine!"
"No, it's not."
"It is, too."
"Who said so?
"Mommy did."
"She did not."
"Yes she did."
"You're a liar."

Sound familiar? These statements are never made in a whisper. The volume and tone can be most irritating. The verbal exchange may deteriorate into fisticuffs.

It's not always necessary to intervene. The kids will ultimately settle it among themselves. You may find them playing a game together soon afterward.

If you feel you must intervene, I suggest you hold court. "Let's settle this dispute the way grownups settle a dispute over property. I'll be the judge, and each of you will tell me your side. There is no shouting in a courtroom. You can't interrupt the other person. If he says something that you feel is wrong, raise your hand and say, 'I object,' and I'll decide whether his statement is right or wrong."

Listen patiently to both sides. You may then say, "In courts the judge does not make a decision right away. He must think about it first. So let me have some time, and when I've reached a decision I'll call you."

Don't rush. Take your time. By the time you hand down a verdict they probably will have forgotten the whole thing. Then you may return the item and tell them you decided to dismiss the case.

You may say, "Where am I going to find time to do all this?" I understand. But if you can't handle it in a way like this, you're better off not intervening. When you intervene, you are in fact acting the part of a judge. If so, play it by the rules.

91.

...AND WHEN WRONG, *PROMPTLY* ADMITTED IT

T his phrase is taken from one of the rules a person must adopt if he wishes to recover from alcoholism or drug addiction. Obviously, this rule is not restricted to these conditions. The wisest thing a person can do is *never to defend a mistake*.

There are so many things we can learn from Torah narratives. King Saul sinned only once, but was not forgiven. King David sinned twice, and was forgiven. Why? Because when the prophet reprimanded David, he immediately said, "I have sinned" (*II Samuel* 12:13). When the prophet reprimanded Saul, he tried to defend his mistake, and only afterward did he admit it (*I Samuel* 15:13-24).

We witnessed the sad incident of a president of the United States resigning. This was not due to a bungled break-in by some of his followers, but to his attempt to cover up the problem. If only he had adhered to the teachings of King Solomon: "One who covers up his sins will not succeed. One who admits and abandons his errant ways will find mercy" (*Proverbs* 28:13).

In my lectures to freshmen medical students I urge them to adopt this teaching. I tell them that I have been involved to a greater or lesser degree with 45,000 patients in my career. I don't know what the statistics are, but I should have been sued for malpractice a number of times. I am far from perfect. I have made mistakes. But I did follow Solomon's teachings, and promptly told the patient and family that I had erred. Solomon was right. They understood.

Within the family, among friends, and even in business, prompt admission of a mistake is far better than defending it. One might think that there can be gain in covering up a mistake. If there is, it is short lived. In the long run, cover-ups do not work.

The great chassidic master, Rabbi Elimelech, used to say that he is confident that he will enter heaven. "On Judgment Day the heavenly tribunal will ask me, 'Did you devote adequate time to Torah study?' I will say, 'No.' 'Did you do *mitzvos* properly?' I will say 'No.' 'Did you commit sin?' I will say, 'Yes.' The tribunal will say, 'He is truthful. He deserves to be in heaven.' "

The most important component of a sincere and lasting relationship is *trust*. Even if one is successful in covering up a mistake, people will sense the dishonesty. Trust is so precious in a relationship that we should never put it in jeopardy.

92.

A TASTE OF HEAVEN

"**H**oney, you know I don't like ... (brussel sprouts, broccoli, asparagus soup, etc.). Why did you make it?"

It makes good sense to prepare foods that everyone likes, but that is not always possible. Several members of the family may have different likes and dislikes. Preparing a nutritious meal with the necessary variety of foods yet suiting everyone's taste may be extremely difficult.

I am reminded of something my mother said. "After 50 years of marriage, I still don't know what foods your father likes or dislikes."

There were some highly spiritual people who were so remote from physical desires that they had no interest whatever in gustatory pleasures. It is not difficult for me to think that my father was among them.

However, I don't think that was necessarily the case. I think my father did like certain foods and may even have had a distaste for others. I think it is an indication of an even higher level of spirituality that he did not make these known to my mother over a 50-year period. Why? Because that might have added just a little extra burden to her chores. As far as he was concerned, she should not have to go out of her way to prepare anything special.

Was this the reason for their happy marriage? No. It was the other way around. The happy marriage was the reason why gustatory considerations were rather unimportant.

What is true of foods is equally true of other physical desires. The happiness of a spiritual relationship may make everything else relatively insignificant.

93.

THE WORLD'S NOT BIG ENOUGH

One of the things that often disrupts household peace is sibling rivalry. "For heaven's sake! What's wrong with these kids? Can't we have a minute of peace in this house?"

Yes. You can have a minute of peace. You can even have a few hours of peace. But don't expect much more. Why? Because brothers and sisters quibble and fight. Managing sibling rivalry may well be the single greatest challenge of parenting.

The theme of sibling rivalry is mentioned three times in Genesis. In all three cases the reason for the intense hatred was jealousy.

"Can't these kids ever be satisfied with what they've got?" Apparently not. Look at Cain and Abel. As the sole heirs of Adam and Eve, they stood to inherit the entire world. "You take Asia, I'll take Africa. You take North America, I'll take South America." No. Not good enough. Cain is jealous of Abel and kills him.

The other two cases involve the jealousy resulting from favoritism. Jacob was his mother's favorite. With her help Jacob

211

received his father's blessings and had to flee for his life from Esau. Joseph was clearly his father's favorite, and he was saved from death only because his brothers rid themselves of him by selling him into slavery.

The Bible is not a history book. It is a guide for proper living. In these cases it teaches us to try to prevent sibling jealousy. Some sibling rivalry may be unavoidable. In his inimitable style, Charles Schulz in his "Peanuts" comic strip has Linus conlude, "Brothers and sisters should never be in the same family." Well, they are in the same family, and there will be rivalry. As long as a child is not made to feel that he is less loved by his parents, the rivalry will not lead to disastrous behavior.

All children are not equal. Look at infants in the newborn nursery and you will see that some personality characteristics are inborn. One child may be brighter or more artistic. One child is born charismatic. Haven't you heard parents say, "Benny was an angel from the day he was born. He never gave me a moment of trouble. Arthur was colicky from day one. He's always had some kind of problem."

Parents are humans. It is only natural for them to have a preference for the child that gives them the most pleasure and the least distress. They may try to conceal this preference, but the less favored child is likely to pick up the vibes.

In contrast to popular belief, we have more control over our emotions than we think. The Baal Shem Tov told a father who complained about his son's behavior, "He is the one who needs your love the most." If one child is superior to another, parents should try and focus on the good points of the disadvantaged child. Perhaps he cannot make straight A's the way his brother does. Look for his strengths and acknowledge them. Reinforce the positives in his personality.

There are some books on parenting that provide ideas for managing sibling rivalry. Looking for guidance to resolve *existing* sibling rivalry is not optimum. Let me repeat. Parenting techniques should be taught to *prospective* parents long before they are confronted with problems.

94

ACCEPT YOUR FEELINGS

Medical science has blessed us with treatments that have doubled the average life span in the past century. The percentage of the elderly in the population is on the increase. However, medicine has not yet found the cure for some of the wear-and-tear conditions. Alzheimer's disease is a dreadful condition which causes families much grief.

In times past, old folks remained in the home. Today, once all the kids are in school it is often necessary for both parents to work to keep the family afloat. There may be no one to remain at home and care for an elderly parent. When an elderly parent is maintained at home, the children may find caring for him or her to be an imposition. Children may feel very guilty for harboring negative feelings. "My father cared for me when I was unable to care for myself. How dare I consider him to be an imposition? How dare I resent having to structure so much of my day around him?"

You know, my friends, an imposition is an imposition. It cannot be comfortable, and there is no point making believe it is.

Handling soiled diapers is unpleasant. You can love the baby to bits, but that doesn't mean you have to make believe that handling the diapers is pleasant.

The same thing is true about caring for a parent. If the parent is living with you and causing some difficulty, you may accept the burden gracefully. There is no point in making believe it is not a burden. You can make a much better adjustment if you realize that it is a burden, but one that you have decided to accept. *The feeling that it is a burden need not detract from your love for the parent.*

I knew a man who cared for his elderly father with great respect and love. He once said, "You know, Dad, I wouldn't give you away for a million dollars. But I wouldn't give five cents for another one of you." He was able to provide loving care even though he recognized that it required some sacrifice on his part.

Denying one's feelings often leads to annoying symptoms. Accepting our feelings and behaving the way we think is proper will be much less demanding on our emotions.

95.

WOULD YOU HAVE COME TO MY FUNERAL?

Feuding, both interfamilial and intrafamilial, is silly and destructive. In the Appalachian Mountains there had once been a fight between a man named Hatfield and another man named McCoy. This turned into a battle for the family honor. Not only did the entire Hatfield family hate everyone in the McCoy family, but also for generations the Hatfields and McCoys were sworn enemies. They were literally out to kill one another, although the reason for the original dispute had long since been forgotten. For people to hate each other for no reason at all is absolutely ridiculous.

It is no less ridiculous when disputes within the family are perpetuated. Two brothers have a disagreement. Some of the siblings and cousins become allies with one of the brothers, while others go to the other side. Not only do the two brothers not resolve their differences, but they also split the family asunder. Relatives are not invited to the weddings of the opposite side.

The only time the two factions may come together is when one of the family dies. Everyone is "invited" to the funeral. How tragic.

Many years ago my cousin invited me to his wedding. As much as I wished to attend, it was just impossible for me to go at that time. My cousin was very upset with me. "Tell me the truth," he said. "If I had died would you have come to my funeral?"

"What kind of silly talk is that?" I asked.

"Just tell me," he said. "Wouldn't you have set aside all the important things and come to the funeral? Just say yes or no."

I couldn't deny it. "O.K.," I said. "I would have come."

"Then does it really bother you that I'm alive? If you could manage to come to my funeral, you can manage to come to my wedding."

He was right. I recall a family which had split into two factions. The father grieved because when there was a wedding in one faction, the other would not attend. He did not have the pleasure of enjoying all his children together.

Then the father died. Yes, both factions attended the funeral. He had finally succeeded in having all his children together at one event.

Unfortunately, he was unable to enjoy it. Could they not have made the same concession while he was alive and able to enjoy it?

The participants in a feud have children of their own. How would they feel if their children would develop animosity toward each other? People should be aware that if they feud, they may be setting an example for their children to behave similarly.

There may be disputes within a family. But they should never be permitted to degenerate into a feud.

217

96

CONFLICTING LOYALTIES

We have deep feelings of loyalty toward our parents. We are also devoted to our spouses. It can really be tough when the interests of the two conflict.

Bella consulted me because she was depressed. Her husband was a busy lawyer, and the time he had for his family was limited. But they did not even have that time, because Charles' mother demanded much of it. Charles had two brothers, but mother rarely called on them. Charles' mother was a widow. She was lonely, and Charles felt he could not refuse her.

For example, they were to take the kids for a whole day picnic one Sunday. Charles' mother called that she needed her lawn mowed and the bushes trimmed. There went the picnic. The children were disappointed, but Charles could not say "no" to his mother.

If they went out for dinner, Charles would invite his mother. The couple were deprived of much needed private time. If she declined the invitation, it was even worse. She would say, "No,

Charles. You go out with Bella. I don't mind being here alone." Charles would choke on every bite. The evening was ruined.

Some people cite the Biblical command, "Honor your father and mother," as giving priority to parents. But long before this, the Bible says, "Therefore shall man leave his father and mother and cleave unto his wife." Parents should indeed be honored, but when children marry, their first responsibility is to the spouse and children.

Charles could have arranged for someone to do the gardening. There were a number of senior activities easily accessible to his mother. She did not have to depend solely on Charles for companionship. In fact, precisely because she depended on him, she avoided making friends. Charles' *kindness* was actually contributing to her loneliness. He should indeed call her and visit her, and accord her the honor due her. But primacy must be given to the wife and children. They are his first responsibility.

When we do what is proper, we should not be guilt ridden. If we are uncertain about our loyalties, we should get competent counseling.

Being torn by conflicting loyalties is tough. But it need not be all that tough. Once we get our priorities in order, we should follow them as directed.

97.

A VERY SHAKY BRIDGE

he problems parents encounter with their teenage children have become the primary focus of current psychology. We often tend to blame outside forces for our misery. The problems of adolescence may be our own fault, i.e., the fault of Western civilization.

I was once called to the emergency room where a confused youngster had come for help. I asked him what his problem was, but received no answer. I sat patiently with him. After a few minutes he said, "I am a nothing."

"Why do you think you are a nothing?" I said.

"What am I?" the young man said. "I'm not a child, and I'm not an adult. I'm a nothing."

Until this moment it had not occurred to me how unnatural the phase of adolescence is. Primitive tribes do not have adolescence. At a particular age young boys and girls undergo a puberty ceremony, and they are then adult men and women. The unsophisticated "primitive" people lived closer to nature and understood it well. A person was either a child or an adult. It was our "advanced" civilization that, much to our regret, concocted the concept of adolescence.

A minor cannot be held responsible for his actions because he lacks the maturity to act responsibly. The parents are therefore held responsible for a minor's actions. The adolescent, however, is too big for the parents to be held responsible. They cannot control him. On the other hand, society has decided that he is not yet mature enough to be held responsible for his actions. Who then is responsible for the actions of an adolescent? No one. Is it any wonder that there is so much adolescent turmoil? The attempt to devise a body of law to govern this unnatural state has been a distinct failure. A 14-year-old may commit the most gruesome crime, but the maximum prison sentence he can be given in some states is four years! At age 18 he is no longer subject to juvenile law.

If things were not bad enough, we have further confused the adolescent. He may become an adult at one age for purchasing liquor, another for cigarettes, yet another for voting, another for driving an automobile, still another for the draft, and yet another to marry. Just across the state line, less than an hour's drive away, there may be a different schedule of ages.

It is well known that it is necessary to have an identity to have a healthy personality. *We have deprived young people of an identity for up to eight years.* The young man in the emergency room was so right. Society has deprived him of a natural identity.

221

"Adolescence" is a contrived state that has no basis in nature.

It might seem that the Bar Mitzvah or Bas Mitzvah at age 13 or 12 might help give young men and women an identity. Alas! We live in a society where the religious distinction has little application. These youngsters are still subject to the hodge-podge schedule, to the non-entity status of their environment.

Adolescence is at best a very shaky bridge between childhood and adulthood. The tragedy is that no bridge was ever necessary. There was no gap to bridge until we made one.

But, you might say, is it realistic to consider 13-year-old youngsters as adults? Well, nature thought so. It made their physiology change at that age instead of at 16 or 18 or 21. Aha! But we wished to outsmart nature. And we have been just as successful tampering with this as we have with the ozone layer.

Do I have a remedy for this sorry state of affairs? No. All I am suggesting is that we understand where these youngsters are coming from. It is not their fault that Western civilization has defied nature.

98.

JUMPING TO CONCLUSIONS

I f we were less certain about our assumptions, we could smooth out many bumps. The problem is that we often project our own ideas onto others, and make conclusions about their behavior based on our ideas.

This sounds very confusing, so let me explain.

To many men, their ability to earn a living is the most important thing in their lives. Their very identity is in being a provider. It is the only thing that justifies their existence.

They may love the wife and children intensely. However, their *identity* may not be as a husband and father. They can think of themselves as a somebody even if they were single. They cannot think of themselves as a somebody if they are not able to earn a living. That's how some men feel.

I have encountered many situations where a wife threatened to leave her husband if he did not stop drinking. "If you loved me and the children you would stop drinking." If the drinking continues, the wife may make good on her threat and leave with the children. Does the husband stop drinking in order to get his family back? Not necessarily.

One day his employer calls him in. His work performance has been slipping. He has been coming to work late. He has called in sick more often, especially on Mondays. He must see the employee assistance counselor. This is a condition for keeping his job. You can bet that he sees the counselor.

After a thorough evaluation, the counselor concludes that the work problems are the result of excessive drinking. He is assured that he can retain his job if he gets treatment for his alcoholism. If he does not and his work performance continues downward, he will lose his job. Does he go for help in order to keep his job? You bet he does.

One might conclude that he did not have enough love for his wife and children, because losing them did not motivate him the way the threat of losing his job did. This is an erroneous conclusion. The man may have loved his family dearly. However, his ego depended on the job, not on the family.

It is a mistake to say that he valued his job more than his family. This is comparing apples and oranges. A person who is drowning and is thrown a rope will hold onto the rope for dear life. There are a thousand things he values more than a rope. However, at this point the rope is what can preserve his life. That is how some men feel about their jobs.

I cite this only as an example of erroneous conclusions. A husband may stay at the office late while the wife is alone at home.

He may take along work on their vacation, which the wife had hoped would give them quality time alone. She may feel hurt that he considers his work more important than being with her. She feels this way because of *her* concept of work. As far as she is concerned, she would be content if her husband made less money and spent more time at home. If the wife understood what earning meant to her husband, she would not think that he does not enjoy her company.

Sometimes the accentuated importance of work may have been the result of early life experiences. Perhaps he experienced the family suffering when he was a child because his father was out of work. Whatever the cause, the fact is that his very essence is dependent on his being able to earn a living.

Emotions do not follow logical reasoning. A woman who will dodge traffic to cross the street may panic and scream when the elevator doors close. She has no fear of oncoming cars but panics in the safety of an elevator! My mother was a highly intelligent person. If she accidentally touched an alpaca garment she would emit a blood-curdling scream.

Emotions are irrational. They are very private. There is no way we can understand how another person may feel, and logical explanations do not alter feelings. This is how we must think about the emotion of being a wage earner. It may defy logic.

Inasmuch as we may not know how and why other people feel, we should not jump to conclusions about their intent. If we interpret their behavior according to *our* feelings, we may make some very incorrect and unfair judgments.

So let's try to avoid drawing conclusions about other people. Let's ask them why they are behaving in a certain way. Let's try to understand others, just as we would want others to try to understand us. In particular, let's not draw conclusions about how our spouse feels toward us by interpreting his/her behavior. We may be making some very unfair judgments.

99.

WHERE ARE YOU GOING?

I have alluded to the importance of having goals in life. It would seem only logical that people should know what they want out of life.

Here too we may be dealing with a side-effect of the scientific and technological advances with which we have been blessed. We have been given so many *things* that we have been distracted from concentrating on goals. Instead, we are more preoccupied with *methods*.

The 1960s witnessed the phenomenon of dethroning G-d. What need is there for G-d when science and technology promise to give us whatever our hearts may desire? People who thought this way did not realize that science and technology can provide only the *how* of living, but not the *why* of life. In fact, the term "teleology" was considered obscene. Science was focused on methods, not on goals. Alas! A life devoid of a goal cannot be a happy one.

The marvels of rapid transportation have given primacy to the method of travel rather than to the destination. It may sound ridiculous, but we are often more concerned with how fast we can get somewhere than with what we will do when we get there. Charles Schulz captured this phenomenon in this charming comic strip.

Right! Many people want to be the first one to get there. Why they want to be there and what they intend to accomplish there are secondary in importance.

My father's counsel was sought by many people. He had few periods of respite when he was not interrupted by a telephone request for help. In those days, travel was by train. There was a high-speed train that made the trip from Chicago to New York in 16 hours. My father avoided that train. Instead, he took the "milk train" that made a stop at every hamlet on the way. This was the only escape he had from the telephone.

Can anyone imagine asking a travel agent today for the *longest* flight rather than the shortest?

We should indeed be grateful for the many conveniences that science and technology have given us. Every day there are new gadgets, some of which actually seem silly. Let us not be so focused on the means of life that we do not give adequate thought to the goal of life.

Other titles by
Rabbi Abraham J. Twerski, M.D.
published by Shaar Press and ArtScroll/Mesorah:

Dearer Than Life
From Bondage to Freedom — A Passover Haggadah
Getting Up When You're Down
Growing Each Day
I am I
It's Not As Tough As You Think
Lights Along the Way
Living Each Day
Living Each Week
Not Just Stories
Positive Parenting (with Ursula Schwartz, M.D.)
Self Improvement? — I'm Jewish!
Smiling Each Day
Twerski on Spirituality
Visions of the Fathers/Pirkei Avos